COPTIC ORTHODOX PATRIARCHATE

See of St. Mark

THE SPIRITUALITY

OF FASTING

BY
H.H. POPE SHENOUDA III

Title	: The Spirituality of Fasting
Author	: H. H. Pope Shenouda III.
Translated by	: Mr. Sobhi Mina Botros
Illustrated by	: Sister Sawsan
Edition	: 1st of October 1990
Typsetting	: J. C. Center
Press	: Dar El Tebaa El Kawmia
Legal Deposit N^o	: 7278/1990
Revised	: COEPA - 1997

H.H. Pope Shenouda III, 117th Pope of
Alexandria and the See of St. Mark

THE SPIRITUALITY OF FASTING

By
H.H. POPE SHENOUDA III

INTRODUCTION

Fasting is an important topic for all, as almost all nations and religions practice some form of fasting. Fasting was even established in man's doctrine before people became different nations. Fasting even goes back to the time of Adam and Eve.

It is not the intention of this book to tackle the subject of fasting from a theoretical point of view but for spiritual benefit.

We aim to discuss the spiritual concepts of fasting and the appropriate conduct during such a period, for our concern is your spiritual growth in God's love.

Many lectures were delivered during and on the subject of fasting. From these, we have selected fifteen to form the topics of this book.

These topics are:
✟ Two lectures about fasting given on 8/8/1969 and 8/15/1969, one at Giza on Saturday 3/8/1970, and one in February 1971.
✟ Two lectures about fasting on 2/22/1974 and 11/29/1974.
✟ Two lectures entitled "Consecrate a fast " on 2/18/1977 and 11/30/1979.

✠ A lecture entitled "A Period of Adherence to God" on 3/4/1977.
✠ Two lectures about Lent in February 1978.
✠ A lecture about Lent on 2/8/1980.
✠ A lecture entitled "We rejoice when we fast" on 5/30/1989.
✠ A lecture on "The Spirituality of Fasting" on 7/3/1981.
✠ A lecture delivered at the Monastery on 2/20/1982.

We have put these lectures in one book, which we hereby present to you.

POPE SHENOUDA III

CHAPTER ONE

THE IMPORTANCE OF FASTING

- ✟ On the Mount of Transfiguration.
- ✟ Fasting, the earliest commandment.
- ✟ Prophets and Apostles fasted.
- ✟ The whole population fasted.
- ✟ Nations fasted.
- ✟ Fasting is a gift
- ✟ Fasting precedes every grace.
- ✟ Fasting precedes Church sacraments.
- ✟ Through fasting, God intervenes.
- ✟ Joy of fasting - a way of life.
- ✟ Fasting and martyrdom.

ON THE MOUNT OF TRANSFIGURATION

The three people, who stood in radiance and glorious light on the Mount of Transfiguration, were people who brought fasting to perfection. For every one of them fasted for forty days and forty nights.

These were:
Our Lord Jesus Christ, may glory be to Him. (Matt 4:2),
Moses (Ex 34:28), and
Elijah (1 Kings 19:8).

This magnificent scene, conceal behind it an important message that is, by conquering the body through fasting, the spirit becomes manifest and the body is transfigured

Our Lord Jesus Christ selected two people who fasted to be with Him on the mount of transfiguration showing their transfigured nature in eternity. Was their body not the same as those who conquered their body through fasting?

What else was said about fasting?

It has been said that:

Fasting is the earliest commandment:

Fasting is the earliest commandment known to mankind, for God commanded our ancestor Adam to refrain from eating a certain fruit from a certain tree (Gen 2:16,17) but allowed him to eat from the rest.

In this way, God set for the body certain limits beyond which it should not go.

Thus, man did not have absolute freedom to take whatever he laid eyes on and whatever he desired. He had to abstain from certain things and control his inclination towards them. Thus since the very beginning, man has had to control his body.
A tree may be "good for food and ... pleasant to the eyes" (Gen 3:6) and yet one must turn away from it.

By abstaining from food, man rises above the level of the body and above matter, and this is the wisdom behind fasting.

Had the first man succeeded in triumphing over his bodily desire for food, and controlled his bodily senses that saw the tree as an appetising sight, it would have proven that his soul had overcome his bodily desires and he would have been worthy to eat from the Tree of Life.

Nevertheless, his own body, which dominated over him, defeated him.

Man went on committing several other bodily sins, one after the other, until he was condemned to walk after the flesh and not the spirit. (Rom 8:1).

Then the Lord Jesus Christ came to restore man to his initial status.

Since man had erred into the sin of eating the forbidden fruit by obeying his body, Christ's first triumph over temptation addressed this particular point, to overcome the desire for food in general and over that which was legitimate.

Christ started His service with fasting, rejecting the devil's temptation to make Him eat to nourish his body. The Lord Jesus Christ showed the devil that man was not a mere body but also a soul nourished by every word that proceeds from the mouth of God. He said to him:

"Man shall not live by bread alone, but by every word that proceeds from the mouth of God." (Matt 4:4).

This was not a new spiritual principal introduced in the New Testament but an old commandment given to man in the first written law. (Dent 8:3).

Thus did Prophets fast:

We hear the Prophet David say*: "I humbled myself with fasting;"* (Ps 35:13*), "I wept and chastened my soul with fasting"* (Ps 69:10), and *"My knees are weak through fasting."* (Ps 109:24). King David also fasted when his son was sick *and "pleaded with God for the child"* lying *"all night on the ground"* (2 Sam 12:16).

The Prophet Daniel fasted (Dan 9:3) and so did the Prophet Ezekiel (Ezek 4:9).

We hear that Nehemiah fasted when he heard that *"The wall of Jerusalem is also broken down, and its gates are burned with fire."* (Neh. 1:3,4). Thus did Ezra, the scribe and priest, fasting and calling upon the whole population to fast. (Ezra 8:2 1).

The prophetess Anna *"did not depart from the temple, but served God with fastings and prayers night and day."* (Luke 2:3 7).

The Apostles also fasted:

As Christ fasted in the New Testament, so did the Apostles who fulfilled the Lord's commandment when He said: "When the bridegroom will be taken away from them, … then they will fast." (Matt 9:15). Thus, the apostle's fast is the oldest and first fast practiced by the Christian Church.

When the apostle Peter was fasting and became so hungry that he longed to eat (Acts 10:10) the vision about the acceptance of gentile nations appeared to him. It was declared to him during his fast about the acceptance of these nations.

In his service to God, the apostle St. Paul said: *"In labours, in sleeplessness, in fastings;"* (2 Cor 6:5), and elsewhere *"In fastings often"* (2 Cor 11:27). It was also said that he and Barnabas fasted together (Acts 14:23).

During the Apostles' fast, the Holy Spirit spoke to them.

Thus the Bible says: "As they ministered to the Lord and fasted, the Holy Spirit said, "Now separate to Me Barnabas and Saul for the work to which I have called them." Then, having fasted and prayed, and laid hands on them, they sent them away." (Acts 13:2,3).

How beautiful then is the Lord's saying to the Apostles about fasting and its relation to casting of devils:
"However, this kind does not go out except by prayer and fasting." (Matt 17:21). Such is the power of fasting, in terrorising devils.

Fasting was not only confined to individuals, but also for whole nations.

Fasting of the whole nations:

This is collective worship (and is other than special individual fasts).

For in doing this, the people's hearts meet together in self-abasement before God.

As Christians pray together with one soul and spirit offering their prayer to God *"with one accord"* (Acts 4:24), and also offer well as their private prayers, so it is with fasting:

There are many examples in the Holy Bible of collective fasts in which all the faithful participated, together and with one spirit, presenting a unified fast to God, the same fast for the whole church.

The most outstanding of these fasts was the one undertaken by the whole population in distress, during the reign of Queen Esther, seeking God's mercy (Esther 4:3,16). They fasted in lamentation and dressed in *"sackcloth with ashes"* until the Lord hearkened and saved them.

Whole population also fasted at a call from Ezra, the priest, by the river Ahava, in humility to God. (Ezra 8:21,23). Together with Nehemiah, they *"Assembled with fasting, in sackcloth, and with dust on their heads."* (Neh 9:1).

In the same way, people fasted in the days of Jehoshaphat (2 Chr 20:3).

The Epistle of Jeremiah tells us of the fasting by the people in the days of Jehoiakim the son of Josiah (Jer 36:9).

There was also another collective fast during the days of the Prophet Joel (Joel 2:12).

Other collective fasts, were *"The fast of the fourth month, The fast of the fifth, The fast of the seventh, And the fast of the tenth"* (Zech 8:19).

Fasting is also common in every religion where nations fast.

Nations also fasted:

An outstanding example of this is the fast of the people of Nineveh (Jon 3) and how God accepted it and forgave their sins.

Another example is the fast of Cornelius the Centurion (Acts 10:30) which God accepted and sent to him the Apostle Peter who preached and baptised him.

The Old Testament tells us about the fast of King Darius during Daniel's ordeal and how he *"spent the night fasting; and no musicians were brought before him."* (Dan 6:18).

Fasting is known in every religion. It was even known in heathen and primitive religions, and indicates that fasting was known before the dispersal of nations and religions.

Anyone reading about Buddhism, Brahmanism, Confucianism, and about Yoga comes across solid examples of fasting and of subduing the body for the soul to take its course. Fasting to them is an exercise for the body and for the soul.

In the life of the famous spiritual leader, Mahatma Gandhi, we see that his fasting was the most manifest and distinctive feature of his life which he often used when faced with problems. Doctors once told him that his blood had started to disintegrate after a long period of fasting.

Through fasting Yogis were able to discover some of the strength of the soul.

Hampered by one's care for the body the strength and power of the soul have only been discovered through fasting.

Hindus believe that the supreme state of Nirvana or the release of the soul from the body to become one with God can only be accomplished through intense asceticism, abstinence, and fasting.

Thus we see that even a soul that is far from the work of the Holy Spirit, and free from bodily desires and its control, becomes a strong, able to attain some of its original natural potential. How much more so is the soul, which is in communion with the Spirit of God?

Fasting is a gift:

When we realise the benefits of fasting, we find that it is a blessing from God.

Yes, fasting is not merely a commandment from God but a godly gift, a grace and a blessing. God the creator of our body and soul knows of our need to fast for its benefit for our spiritual life, development and our eternity. He granted us the knowledge and manner of fasting. As a kind Father and a wise Teacher, He has recommended fasting for us.

Fasting precedes every grace and service:

Through fasting, we prepare ourselves to receive every blessing that God offers us.

Feasts bear for us certain blessings. This is why fasting precedes every feast.

Communion bears for us a special blessing. That is why we fast to be ready for it.

Priestly ordainment bears a blessing. That is why we receive it with fasting. Thus, the bishop who undertakes the ordainment fasts, the candidate for it also fasts, and all others who participate in these prayers.

At the time of our forefathers the disciples, the selection of deacons was accompanied with fasting: *"As they ministered to the Lord and fasted, the Holy Spirit said, "Now separate to Me Barnabas and Saul "* And "having fasted and prayed, and laid hands on them" (Acts 13:2,3).

Fasting also precedes service:

Before the Lord Jesus Christ started His overt service, He fasted for forty days, spending the time in seclusion with the Father on the mountain

We likewise, after ordaining a new priest, assign to him a period of forty days of fasting and seclusion, usually at a monastery, before he begins his service.

Our fathers, the Apostles, began their service by fasting when they received the Holy Spirit, and it accompanied their spiritually acceptable service.

A deacon fasts to grow spiritually, to receive God's help and soften God's heart to join him in his service

We also see in the life of John the Baptist that he lived a life fasting and seclusion before his call for people to repent.

Fasting is not for service alone but **also precedes the Church sacraments:**

✠ A person is required to fast to receive **the sacrament of baptism**. Their godfather and the priest also fast to greet this new spiritual birth.
✠ Fasting proceeds the **sacrament of Chrism**, the acceptance of the Holy Spirit.
✠ **Congregations also fast to receive the sacrament of the Eucharist** or Communion.
✠ **The sacrament of the Unction of the sick** (the prayer on the oil) is performed by a fasting priest. Those anointed with the oil of this sacrament also have to be fasting. Patients however, who are unable to fast and those absolved from fasting for the sacrament of communion, are exempt.
✠ The **sacrament of priesthood,** is practiced while fasting as mentioned earlier.
✠ What remain are the **sacrament of confession** and the **sacrament of marriage**.

How marvellous it would be for those who came to confess their sins while fasting and repentant. However, since the Church seeks the sinners regardless of their state, it has not set fasting as a condition for this sacrament.

As for the sacrament of marriage, Jesus Christ exempted it, saying: *"Can the friends of the bridegroom fast while the bridegroom is with them?"* (Mark 2:19). However, the early ascetic church practiced the sacrament of marriage after the raising of the morning incense at which time the bride and groom fasted to receive the Holy Communion, and went on fasting for the remainder of the day. Nowadays, this practice is uncommon.

The faithful, who fast, gain the blessings of the Holy Spirit during the Church sacraments.

In the same way, the Church recognised the importance of fasting in the life of worship and service. It has also known it in times of hardship and has come up with a spiritual rule which is:

Through fasting, God intervenes:

We can cite some examples including: Nehemiah, Ezra, Daniel, Queen Esther interceding for her people, the Church in the fourth century in the depths of Arius's heresy and on many other through the generations, people fasted and God intervened.

The Fraction prayer of Lent, concentrates on the importance of fasting as an established creed in the conscience of the Church, knowing that through faith and fasting problems are solved.

The unwise man has confidence in his power and intelligence but he who is aware of his weakness appeals to God through fasting when in trouble.

Through his fast, he humbles himself before God and seeks His mercy, saying: *"Arise O Lord God"*. The Lord answers him through the words in the Psalm: *"For the oppression of the poor, for the sighing of the needy, Now I will arise," says the Lord; "I will set him in the safety for which he yearns."* (Ps 12:5).

Fasting is a time to let God know of our every problem. It is a period for the contrite heart to lament and for God to hear.

It is a time when people come close to God. A time when God comes close, listens to their yearning and lamentations and acts.

As long as people are preoccupied with their desires, lusts of the body and materialistic things, they feel that God stands far away from them. However, it is not He who detaches Himself from us but we, who push Him away rejecting Him and refusing to approach Him.

On the other hand, during a fast intermingled with prayer, man draws near to God and says to Him: Lend a hand to Your worshipper.

It is the heart crying to God that He may intervene in his life.

This may take place at any time, but it becomes more profound, more sincere and more powerful during the period of fasting.

Through true fasting man can soften God's heart.

He, who realises the benefits of fasting and its effectiveness in his life as well as in his relationship with God, rejoices over it.

Joy of Fasting:

We are not of the type of people who fast and, while fasting, long for the time to break our fast. On the contrary, when we are not fasting we long for the time when fasting will return.

A spiritual person rejoices over the periods of fasting more than he does over feast days during which he eats and drinks. Many are those who long for fasting during the fifty-day period that follows Easter and during which there is neither fasting or continual prostration. Their longing for fasting increases so strong that they rejoice at the arrival of the Apostles' fast having been deprived of the joy of fasting during the preceding fifty days.

Those who are spiritual rejoice so much at fasting that general fasts are not sufficient for them. Thus, they urge their father confessors to allow them to add their own additional fasts. They support their request with the argument that their spiritual condition becomes stronger during the period of fasting, their health improves and that their bodies become lighter.

Those who claim that fasts should be shortened and reduced in number attest to the fact that they have neither experienced the joy of fasting nor known its benefits.

God willing, we shall discuss in the coming chapters the benefits of fasting as the source of joy for the spiritual and the lifestyle for the monks.

A way of life:

So loved was fasting to our fathers the monks, that they made of it their lifestyle.

They fast, with the exception of feast days their whole life. They did not suffer from physical fatigue but discovered in it spiritual delight, found satisfaction and became accustomed to it.

It was once said that on one occasion, at the advent of Lent in the desert, a herald was sent calling upon monks and drawing their attention to the sacred fast. When one of the elders heard the herald's exhortation, he said to him: "Son, what is it this fast you are talking about? I am not aware of it because all my days are the same. (Ie. that all of them are days of fasting)."

Saint Paula the anchorite used to eat only half a loaf of bread at sunset.

Some monks used to fast every day until sunset like a holy monk who once said; "Thirty years have passed by during which the sun has not seen me eating".

Some monks used to fast for days. Saint Makarius the Alexandrian, for example, fasted though out the year and ate only once week during the Holy Lent, while visiting the Monasteries of Saint Pachomius.

The fasting of our fathers, were not confined to specific periods, or the length of time, but also as form of monasticism, applied it to the kind of food they ate.

Abba Nofer, the anchorite, ate dates from a palm tree at his place of seclusion. Saint Moses the anchorite, as well as Saint Pigimy, another anchorite, ate desert grass and drank from the morning dew.

Consistent fasting regulated the lives of the Fathers.

This lifestyle of a monk becomes comforting and harmonious for both the body and the soul. A stable lifestyle, to which they become accustomed which regulates their lives

As for the pitied laymen, they sway from one extreme to another when fasting. They deprive themselves of food only to break their fast to partake of anything they desire.

They abstain for a while, to allow themselves what they want for another period, then go back to indulgence, thus they sway between abstention and indulgence. They build, then destroy, and then build again, only to demolish again without recovery.

True fasting is to train oneself in self-control, to follow for the rest of your life.

Self-control becomes a blessing for his life, not only during the time of fasting when we change the time and the food we eat, but also during the normal days.

In this context, fasting is not a punishment but a blessing.

Confessor fathers used to impose as a sever form of punishment for their spiritual sons, to break their fast early, to eat meat or appetising foods. This was done in order to abase their spiritual son's proud heart that thinks of itself to have become a hermit or an ascetic. He would thus bring down his arrogance by making him eat and feel abased to rid him of thoughts of vain glory.

Fasting and Martyrdom:

It is natural that he, who cannot abstain from food, would find it difficult to offer his life.

Through continuous training and negligence for the bodily needs, a courageous soul is trained to endure hunger and thirst, bring the body into subjection to conquer the desires and lusts of the body. It is able to endure the hardships of imprisonment and the pain of torture. These people were able through God's grace, to offer their bodies up to death at the time of martyrdom.

Thus fasting became the training of the spiritual school of martyrs, not only in the physical sense, but also from the spirituality gained in fasting. Days of fasting are not only for our spiritual deeds, repentance, and coming closer to God, but they also help evoke our love for eternity with Him. Man therefore harbours no fear when faced with death since he is prepared for it. Rather, man is happy that he is to rid himself of his body to meet with God. As St. Paul says: *"...having a desire to depart and be with Christ, which is far better."* (Phil 1:23).

Through fasting, the Church trained its children for the ascetic life.

Through asceticism, they are trained to renounce the world and become martyrs.

Martyrs were mostly those who lived a life of fasting, prayer, and asceticism. As the Apostle Paul said: *"And those who use this world as not misusing it. For the form of this world is passing away."* (1 Cor 7:31).

CHAPTER TWO

FASTING AND THE BODY

✝ Definition of fasting.
✝ Period of abstinence.
✝ The element of hunger.
✝ Fasting as connected to vigil.
✝ Kind of food.
✝ Vegetarian food.
✝ Bodily benefits of fasting.
✝ Fasting is not a mere bodily virtue.

Definition of fasting:

The spiritual definition of fasting will be mentioned later in detail.

However, what are the physical aspect of the definition of fasting?

Fasting is abstinence from food, for a period, followed by eating food free from animal fat.

Period of abstinence:

A period of abstinence is essential, since we would simply be vegetarians if we ate without observing it from the beginning of the day. The word fasting means abstinence or cessation. It is therefore necessary to refrain from eating for a certain period of time.

The length of abstinence varies from one person to another. The following outlines some of the reasons for this:

1   People differ in their spirituality. A beginner for example, cannot abstain for a long time when compared with the well trained or the spiritually mature who can abstain for a long time. An anchorite is able to fast for days in the same manner of our fathers the monks, the hermits, and the anchorites.

2   Those who fast differ in age. The ability of a child or a boy to fast differs from that of a young or grown-up man, and is also differs for the elderly.

3   Those who fast also differ in their state of health. A strong
    person may endure more than the physically weak.
    Moreover, the sick may require special treatment, and may
    be exempt from abstinence in accordance with their ailment
    and the treatment required.

4   Those who fast also differ in the type of work they do.
    Some work requires great physical effort, while others work
    in an office environment sitting down at their desks for a
    number of hours. The first differs from the latter in their
    endurance to abstain from food.

5   Fasting requires a gradual progression. One should fast by
    gradually increasing the length of abstinence over the period
    of the fast. The spiritual fathers usually recommend this
    useful method.

There is however a minimum time of abstinence, which
varies depending on the fast. The minimal fast period for Lent
should be higher than for the rest of the fasts and the minimum
during the Passion Week is higher than that of Lent. Some are
able to fast from Maundy Thursday up to the Easter Mass and
others on the day preceding Christmas or Epiphany. As for the
weak, their endurance is limited.

Despite all this, we need to set the following important rule:

**The period of abstinence should be under the guidance of
your Father confessor.** Excessive periods of fasting may
become detrimental to the body and possibly to the soul as it
falsely instils the notion of false glory. On the other hand, some
may become lax and lose the benefits of fasting. It is best to

seek the guidance of your Father confessor on this matter.

However from the Church's point of view, on the period of abstinence, we would like to pose the following question:

Is there any association between abstinence from eating and the ninth hour?

There is in fact some connection, for in the Church rite of the ninth hour prayers, we observe the selection of the Bible chapter, which deals with blessing of food after a period of hunger. (Luke 9:10-17).

In the ninth hour prayer, we remember the death of our Lord Jesus Christ on the cross. Why then is this passage? It appears that abstinence was communally practiced until the ninth hour and thus this passage was suitably placed to allow people to pray then eat their food.Since days of fasting cover the major portion of the year. This bible chapter has remained for all year long to remind us of fasting, even during the days when there is no abstinence to allow us to maintain our daily prayers and remember God's blessing of food before we eat.

The ninth hour of the day actually coincides with three o'clock in the afternoon since the first hour of the day corresponds to six o'clock in the morning.

In any case, there is no need to elaborate further on this point since the period of abstinence differs from one person to another. The period of abstinence is left up to the Father confessor and to the spiritual condition of the person fasting.

What is important is the spiritual aspect of the period of abstinence. It is far more important to discuss the method by which man may benefit spiritually from his abstinence than on the formalities and laws that govern the period of abstinence. A person may not benefit spiritually if they follow a non-spiritual method, even if he abstains from food until the ninth hour or even sunset.

What is, therefore, the spiritual way?

1 **The period of abstinence must be one of renunciation and asceticism** caring not for the body. You should therefore not think about when and what you will eat while abstaining from food, nor find pleasure in preparing what you will eat. On the contrary, the period of abstinence should be a time when you elevate yourself totally above the levels of eating, materialism, and food.

2 **After the period of abstinence, do not eat greedily,** for he who abstains from food, then eats what he covets, or chooses certain foods that he enjoys, has not subdued his body, humiliated it, nor rid it of its lusts. This indicates that he has not benefited spiritually from the period of abstinence, a time of renunciation and asceticism if he greedily eats what he lusts for. Look at what the Prophet Daniel said about his fast: *"I ate no pleasant food."* (Dan 10:3).

It is like he who demolishes what he has built... all in vain! Fasting is not to build then demolish, and build again only to demolish, without the desire for growth!

3 **Do not wait in anticipation for the end of the abstinence period as to what you will eat.**

Do not hasten to eat when the time comes. Try if you can to resist even for a few minutes and wait. When it is time to eat, say to yourself: Let us pray for a while, then eat, or let us read a book and contemplate for some time, then eat.

Do not pounce on food. Let renunciation that you harboured during abstinence continue to be with you after you have eaten, for this is spiritually beneficial and you will be rewarded.

Let the spirit not the hour guide you.

Elevate yourself above food, material things and the body in-order to move forward to the depth of abstinence.

As for the period and time of abstinence, it would be beneficial if it led you to the feeling of hunger.

Let us here talk to you about the element of hunger in fasting:

The element of hunger:

Many abstain from food, then eat without feeling or enduring hunger. They are without patience to profit from fasting spiritually. The Bible presents to us many examples of hunger during fasting.

Jesus Christ, as well as the Apostles, fasted until they became hungry.

The bible mentions that after Jesus Christ fasted for forty days that: *"afterward He was hungry."* (Matt 4:2).
According to the account of Saint Luke: *"And in those days He ate nothing, and afterward, when they had ended, He was hungry."* (Luke 4:2). Jesus Christ also became hungry on Easter Monday. (Mark 11: 12).

However, some may argue that Christ's fasting is difficult and beyond us. Therefore, let us talk about the fasting of ordinary people who experienced the element of hunger.

It was said about the Apostle St Peter that: *"He became very hungry, and would have eaten "* (Acts 10:10). In the discourse of St Paul and his companions' service, he said: *"In weariness and toil, in sleeplessness often, in hunger and thirst, in fasting often…"* (2 Cor 11:27). He also said: *"learned both to be full and to be hungry."* (Phil 4:12).

God blessed the condition of hunger, saying:

"Blessed are you who hunger now, For you shall be filled."(Luke 6:11).

If Lazarus's hunger qualified him to embrace our Father Abraham for his share of trouble on earth though it had not been of his own free will, how much more grace will God give to those in eternity who willingly hunger ascetically seeking Him.

God prepared His people in the wilderness through hunger.

He said to those people: "And you shall remember that the Lord your God led you all the way these forty years in the wilderness…So He humbled you, allowed you to hunger, and fed you with manna which you did not know nor did your fathers know, that He might make you know that man shall not live by bread alone; but man lives by every word that proceeds from the mouth of the Lord." (Dent 8:2,3).

He who escapes from the statement: *"He humbled you, allowed you to hunger"* will have the statement: *"fed you with manna"* in the wilderness evade him.

However, the children of Israel perished in the wilderness when they murmured and became hungry.

Fasting acquires its perfection in toleration to hunger.

If you do not become hungry, you will not understand the depth and meaning of fasting, and if you do not prolong or endure your fast and eat directly after your abstinence, you will not be awarded the benefits conveyed by hunger.

What then are the spiritual benefits conveyed by hunger?

He who hungers becomes aware of his weakness.

Thus he defeats his sense of self-delusion, from self reliance and excessive self-confidence. Bodily humility and weakness leads him to spiritual submission.

When the body is humbled, the soul is humbled, feeling the need for support and pleads to God for strength, saying: O Lord, support my weakness with Your Godly power for I by myself can do nothing.

Man's prayer is intense when hungry.

Fervent spiritual prayers do not come from a full stomach.

That is why prayer and fasting are inseparable. People fast when they seek depth in their prayer. Prayers and bible readings during Passion Week become profound when united by hunger...

Easter melody recording during Passion Week exhibits spiritual depth by he who records it while fasting. A recording of the same melody on other than fasting days, loses its spiritual depth to become in all probability a mere tune.

God desires that through hunger that man may identify his weakness. Prostration is therefore more effective when hungry than with a stomach filled with food.

My advice to you is this: If you feel hungry, resist for a while the temptation to eat so that you may receive the blessing of hunger.

The Lord Jesus Christ fasted for forty days and finally became hungry. When the Devil tempted Christ to eat He refused despite His hunger. In doing so, He taught us a lesson. Therefore, endure your hunger, and do not avoid it.

Do not escape from the feeling of hunger through idle talk, wasting of time or sleep which you may resort to in order to overcome the period of hunger without feeling it. By escaping from hunger, you forfeit its blessings, spiritual benefits and the virtue of endurance and control over the body.

Our aim is to benefit from hunger and not escape from it.

If hunger presses on you, say to yourself that you do not deserve to eat.

Say to yourself: I do not deserve to eat because of my sins. You become inwardly humble when you are physically fatigued which allows you to pray in humility and help you to relinquish pride, vanity and self-complacency.

As for he who stands to pray in might, health and the strength of iron, where will submissiveness come from?

Two minutes prayer whiles hungry are better than hours when full.

In fact, a hungry person longs for prayer, while he who is full often forgets. That is why most faithful people pray before eating.

Peruse hunger in wisdom when you fast.

Those who have experienced the spiritual benefit arising from hunger tend to prolong its period. However, one must be careful not to exaggerate in utter exhaustion that you end up too frail to stand on your feet to pray. Such a person may opt to pray while prostrating not out of submissiveness but to seek comfort and relaxation for his tired body.

Be wise to train yourself within your body's limit of endurance. However, I have a frank word to say to you:

Do not be afraid of hunger, for it is a passing sensation. The reason is that the more you give your stomach, the more it expands to accommodate more. Moreover, in cases of those who are overweight, the stomach is flabby, its walls are weak, and if you do not fill it, you feel hungry.

If you endure your hunger, your stomach will re-condition itself and contract. If you persist, it will no longer be in need for much. Hunger will then not persist since a small quantity will give the stomach a feeling of fullness.

A wise person is one who controls his stomach. He does not eat so much that his stomach becomes flabby, and does not over deprive it of food to make it shrink to a size unfit for the needs of his body.

Moderation in this matter is useful and wise.

Fasting and Wakefulness:

Being filled with food leads to heaviness of the body and consequently to sleep. As for he who fasts, his body is light, his system is not burdened with the processes of digestion, and is able to stay awake until late.

Fasting coupled with watchfulness leads to brightness of thought.

All the saints who perfected fasting were famous for their vigil. We also see that the disciples' eyes grew heavy in the orchard after the two dinners that they could not sit up with the Lord even for one hour. (Matt 26:40).

It is not in your favour my brother that the bridegroom should come at midnight to find you sleeping. The Bible says, *"Blessed are those servants whom the master, when he comes, will find watching"*(Luke 12:37).

Therefore, train yourself to fast in alertness and watchfulness so that you can spend the night in prayer with God.

Kind of Food:

I have talked about hunger and the period of abstinence, what remains is the topic of what are the different types of food appropriate for fasting. It is useful to remember of what the Prophet Daniel said about his fast:
"I ate no pleasant food" (Dan 10:3).

Therefore, if you fast but still give your body what it craves for, then in truth you had not fasted. Thus, distance yourself from things that you crave so that you may overcome your body and subject it to your will. Do not seek special food or ask for it to be prepared in the manner that you like. If an item is placed before you which you have not ordered but which you like, do not eat much of it

I would like to remind you of our saintly fathers who said, "If food you crave is placed before you, spoil it a little then eat it".

By spoiling it, he may have meant, for instance, that you add something to it to alter its taste.

At least, do not eat all that is offered to you of the kind of food you crave. As one of the fathers said: "Conclude your meal while you still crave it", meaning that your body wishes to go on eating that kind of food while you try to control yourself and stay away from it.

Here we face many questions posed by some people:

Can vegetables and margarine be consumed when fasting? Is soya cheese acceptable? Should we or should we not eat fish during a particular fast? What do you think of non-dairy chocolate? Etc.

These questions can be resolved in one way by examining the ingredients or contents of these foods. On the other hand, these questions should also be viewed from a spiritual point of view: For example, vegetable fat, is merely polyunsaturated, but if you eat it because of your craving for fatty food, then the matter becomes different. Literally speaking, you would be fasting, but you would not be benefiting spiritually.

We do not want to keep to the formalities of fasting alone. The same applies to Soya cheese. One may argue whether or not it contains if it contains ingredients of animal source. However, from a spiritual point of view, do you love cheese so much that you insist on gratifying your bodily desires during the fast by finding a substitute or an alternative? The same applies to non-dairy chocolate; do you crave that brand in particular? Why not substitute it with a cup of cocoa?

As for fish, it is primarily animal food. Although it has been permitted for the weak who cannot endure the large number of fasts, it is not permitted in first class fasts.

However, if your body craves fish while fasting, do not eat any.

This does not only apply to fish, but to anything that you may crave in order to control your desires when fasting, even if it may be permitted.

Is not marriage lawful? Yet, those who fast stay away from sexual intercourse while fasting in order to have self control. (1Cor 7:5). The Gentile King, Darius did the same. (Dan 6:18).

Vegetarian Food:

We have discussed the period of abstinence and the element of hunger in fasting. Now we would like to talk about vegetarian food as a God's divine way since the beginning since Adam and Eve and up to the descendants of Noah were vegetarian.

God created a vegetarian man.

Adam and Eve, while in Paradise, ate nothing but plants, beans and fruit. As God said to them, *"I have given you every herb that yields seed which is on the face of all the earth, and every tree whose fruit yields seed; to you it shall be for food"* (Gen 1:29).

Man also remained vegetarian after his exile from Paradise.
However, man was permitted, along with the beans and fruit, to eat from the herbs of the land, i.e. vegetables. Thus, when he sinned, God said to him: *"And you shall eat the herb of the field. "* (Gen 3:18).

We have not heard that our Father, Adam, and our Mother, Eve, fell ill because of malnutrition. On the contrary, we hear that Adam, a vegetarian, lived 930 years. (Gen 5:5). So were also the lives of his sons and grandsons who were vegetarian. (Gen 5)

Man did not eat meat except after Noah's Ark. This took place at a dismal time when "the wickedness of man was great in the earth" and so, "the Lord was sorry that he had made man on the earth, and it grieved Him at His heart" (Gen 6:5-6) and He submerged the whole world with the flood.

After the flood water subsided, God said to our Father Noah and his sons: "Every moving thing that lives shall be food for you. I have given you all things, even as the green herbs. But you shall not eat flesh with its life, that is, its blood."(Gen 9:3-4).

When God led His people into the wilderness, He fed them with manna. "And it was like white coriander seed, and the taste of it was like wafers made with honey."(Ex 16:31). "The people went about and gathered it, ground it on millstones or beat it in the mortar, cooked it in pans, and made cakes of it; and its taste was like the taste of pastry prepared with oil." (Num 11:8).

But when He allowed them to eat meat, He did it in anger.

God consented to their request because of their craving for meat. God granted their wish but punished them for it. "But while the meat was still between their teeth, before it was chewed, the wrath of the Lord was aroused against the people, and the Lord struck the people with a very great plague. So he called the name of that place Kibroth Hattaavah, because there they buried the people who had yielded to craving." (Num 11:33-34).

Daniel and his companions also ate vegetables.

They ate vegetables (Dan 1:12) and were determined in their hearts not to defile themselves with the King's meat and wine. (Dan 1:8).

We see the Prophet Daniel say while fasting: *"I ate no pleasant food, no meat or wine came into my mouth, nor did I anoint myself at all, till three whole weeks were fulfilled."* (Dan 10:3).

Ezekiel also ate vegetarian food while fasting.

He did this in obedience to a Godly order from God who said to him: *"Also take for yourself wheat, barley, beans, lentils, millet" and spelt."* (Ezek 4:9).

Vegetarian food is light, lean and soothing.

It has nothing of the heaviness, grease or fat of meat or whatever effect it may have on one's body. We observe for example that savage animals are carnivorous while the tame ones are herbivorous. Vegetarian people tend to be calmer in nature than meat-eaters. Does it not make you wonder that most of the animals we eat, such as cattle, sheep and fowls, are herbivorous.

These herbivorous animals are not weak due to eating such food.

Moreover, we describe a strong man saying that he has the health of a camel or a horse both of which are vegetarian. Matadors, who practiced bullfighting, displayed their strength by confronting a powerful bull, a herbivorous animal. We can then conclude that eating plant food does not weaken the body.

Vegetarians, including hermits and anchorites, lived a long life.

Bernard Shaw, the famous writer, was vegetarian, lived for 94 years, and suffered no ailment throughout his life. How many others can we attribute their long life to being vegetarians?

Saint Paul, the first of the anchorites, lived as a hermit for eighty years without seeing a man's face, and so he lived to be around hundred. The majority of anchorites also lived long lives. Not only were they vegetarians, but also lived a life of asceticism and ate little. Nevertheless, they enjoyed good health. Saint Antonius, the father of all monks, lived to be 105 years old. His life was one of continuous fasting and yet he enjoyed good health and used to walk tens of miles without becoming tired

I do not want to concentrate too much on the scientific aspects of vegetarian food, but the spiritual ones as has been in the life of man since Adam.

It is true that principal amino acids abound more in animal than in vegetable protein. However vegetable protein has sustained and kept healthy monks, vegetarians and those mentioned above.

We should also not forget that the Church allows fish in some fasts, which of course, contains animal protein. Moreover, there are long non-fast periods.

Therefore, do not be afraid of fasting, for it is of benefit to the body.

The benefits of fasting to the Body:

Fasting benefits the body in several ways, some of which are outlined below:

1. **Fasting is a period of rest for some of the organs of our body.** It is a period of rest for all the digesting and associated systems, such as the stomach, the intestines, the liver, and the gall bladder, overworked by high consumption and composite food. The digestion system become upset when more food is introduced as it attempts to digest the existing contents.

   Conversely, when one fasts, the digestion system rests during the period of abstinence, and the light food, which is later eaten, does not trouble it. Moreover, we find relief from the food we eat between meals. How wonderful it would be to carry this discipline over to non-fasting days.

2. Another benefit of **vegetarian foods** is that it reduces **cholesterol,** since it is well documented that fats and grease found in meat leads to an increase in the blood cholesterol level. The danger is of course in the formation of blood clots. As a result, doctors ask their patients to keep away from food such as meat, eggs, fatty oils and the like in order to keep the body healthy, especially for those advanced in years. They recommend vegetable foods in an attempt to revert man to his original vegetarian nature, to the food of the Garden of Eden.

Another benefit of fasting for the body is that:

3. One who fasts gets rid of his obesity and flabbiness:

When a person is overweight, the heart is overworked as it attempts to send blood to the extra quantity of tissue in the form of excess fat. This extra quantity of tissue is beyond that which God has required him to support. In addition, obesity causes many ailments to the body.

Doctors insist that body weight be reduced to keep it healthy. They impose certain regimes upon an obese person (which is considered a sickness), to control what he eats instead of eating uncontrollably.

One who fasts and controls himself is not in need of a special diets.

Fasting, in the spiritual sense, is far superior to physical treatment, for it treats the spirit, the body, and the soul all together.

If a person fasts out of his love for God for a spiritual gain, his body automatically benefits, which is better than fasting on doctor's order to reduce body weight. It is indeed a tragedy to see people spend a large part of his life putting on weight, then spend another part of their life trying to get rid of excess body fats.

If he or she had been moderate, and had known from the start the value and benefit of fasting, he would not have had the need to exert all that effort in gaining weight and later trying to loose it.

This reminds me of a woman who goes on eating until her body loses its beautiful symmetry. Then, when doctors advise her to fast, to reduce her consumption, and follow a strict diet, she does so, not for God but for the beauty of her body. Thus, she does not eat, but she does not receive the blessing of fasting, for what she does is not done out of love for God!

Would it not have been more beneficial for these people to have fasted both for their bodily health and at the same time for their spirit to soar high and approach God?

Fast then for God, before you are compelled to fast for medical reasons without any spiritual benefit to you.
One of the benefits of fasting and, in particular the period of abstinence and hunger, is that:

4. Fasting helps treat many illnesses:

One of the most important books I have read in this field is the one entitled "Treatment by Fasting" written by the Russian scientist Alexi Soforin and translated into Arabic in 1930.

This scientist remarks that fasting helps rid the body of its toxins. Although the body gets rid of many of them through its various methods of excretion, some remain and may be excreted through fasting...

The scientist also states that in fasting the body does not get enough food and begins to dissipate its fats, grease, diseased and festered tissues, which are excreted by the body.

This scientist also found out that a long term temperate fast that followed a certain regime could treat many diseases.

I hereby present his research for study as a scientist who tested the contents of his book.

Are there any other bodily benefits through fasting? Yes.

5. Fasting makes the body light and active:

Our fathers, who perfected fasting, had light bodies and elevated spirits. They were energetic, having strong hearts and were able to walk tens of kilometres a day without becoming tired. They moved in the wilderness like deer, and their minds were not sluggish but very bright. Thus through fasting they gained strength for their bodies, spirits, and minds. They found comfort and pleasure in fasting, so much so that their life became a life of fasting.

6. Let nobody therefore deceive you and say that fasting or vegetable food weakens one's health, for in fact it gives it strength.

Fasting is not a remedy for the spirit alone, but it is also for the body. There have never been any cases were vegetarian food has harmed or weakened anyone.

Daniel and the three young men did not eat meat at the King's table. It was sufficient to eat beans and their health was better than the others. (Dan 1: 15).

Our fathers, the ascetics and the great monks, were very strict in their fasts. Yet we have never heard that fasting weakened their health. On the contrary, they remained strong even in their old age.

No-where is it mentioned that our father Adam became sick or weak from eating vegetarian food. The same applies to Eve and to all the fathers preceding Noah's and the great flood. Therefore, rest assured about your bodily health.

What tires the body is not fasting but eating.

Overeating, indigestion, eating between meals, etc… all leads to bodily exhaustion. Moreover, the body is also fatigued from the extra heat energy generated by foods consumed beyond man's need. How great are the sicknesses brought about by overeating.

Therefore, you have to liberate yourselves from the idea that fasting hurts your health.

Nursing mothers incorrectly assume out of their love and concern for the health of their children, that they must be chubby and full. They assume that this is a sign of good health although an overweight person is weaker in health than a slim one.

Wrong motherly affection is used to prevent children from fasting or discouraged. We say that this affection is erroneous because it did not concern itself with the son's soul as it did with his body, as if they are only responsible for their sons' bodies only. In their concern for their children's bodily health, they neglect the nourishment of their souls.

Despite this, saintly children used to fast.

An example of these is given by Saint Mark, the hermit on Mount Antonius, who started fasting in his early childhood and kept on fasting through out his life.

Likewise was Saint Shenouda, the father of hermits, who at the age of nine, used to give his food away to shepherds and pray standing up while fasting, till sunset.

To the young and old, fasting bestows health and strength. It freed their bodies from their extra fat and water.

Many saintly bodies have kept from decay, all because of God's blessing that preserved them as a reward for their faithfulness. On the other hand, because their bodies had little in the way of fat and dampness, the causes of decay.

Meat can be preserved without decay for a long time if it is exposed to heat which rids it of its water content and dissolves its fat which dries it up and preserve it. To the some extent were the bodies of saints who, through fasting were without fat and excess water. Thus, decay could not touch them.

However, why should we concentrate on the body? Is fasting a virtue for the body alone?

Fasting is not a mere bodily virtue:

Fasting is not merely a virtue for the body apart from the soul, because any virtue requires the participation of the soul.

What then is the role of the body in fasting? And what is the role of the soul?

True fasting is a spiritual act primarily taking place inside the heart.

The function of the body in fasting is to prepare the soul or rather to disclose the soul's affection.

The soul rises above the level of materialism and food, and above the level of the body. It leads the body along in victorious

45

procession and spiritual desires. The body expresses this through fasting.

If we confine our definition of fasting to the humiliation of the body through hunger and deprivation of what it covets, we will be adhering to the negative aspect of fasting, ignoring the positive and spiritual ones.

Fasting is not hunger for the body but nourishment for the soul.

Fasting, as some people speculate, is not a bodily torture, martyrdom, or a cross, but it is a way to elevate the body to reach the level of cooperation with the soul. When we fast, our intention is not to torture the body but to shun its behaviour. Thus, one who fasts becomes a spiritual and not a physical person.

Fasting is an ascetic soul which takes the body with it as its partner in asceticism.

Fasting is not a hungry body but an ascetic one.

Fasting is not bodily hunger but bodily elevation and purity. It is not a body that hungers and longs for food, but a body that rids itself of the desire to eat.

Fasting is a time when the soul flourishes and lifts the body up with it.

It rids the body of its loads and burdens and lifts it up so that God may work with it without impediment to the happiness of the spiritual entity.

Fasting is a spiritual time spent together by the body and soul performing a spiritual act. The body and the soul join in doing the work of the soul, ie. praying, meditating, praising and coming in communion with God.

We do not pray only with a fasting body but also with a fasting soul, mind and heart abstaining from lusts and desires. The soul also abstains from love of the passing world. All for the sake of living with God, nourished and loved by Him.

A fast in this way is the proper vehicle for spiritual deeds, a spiritual atmosphere to live in his heart, spirit, soul, thought, senses, and emotions with God.

Fasting is the bodily expression of abstinence from materialism and the longing for a life with God. Through abstinence, the body joins the soul in its aspects of spiritual work. Through this, the body becomes spiritual in attitude and takes on the appearance of the soul.

In spiritual fast, neither the soul nor the spiritual body, is anxious about bodily wants.

Care not for the body:

In the Lord's discourse on spiritual nourishment, we hear Him says: *"Do not labor for the food which perishes, but for the food which endures to everlasting life."* (John 6:27). He then continued by talking about the true bread from Heaven the bread of God, and the bread of life. (John 6:32-35). Here He appeals to the soul for its nourishment and our thoughts to the spiritual way so as not to occupy our minds with the body and its needs.

When Christ said that *"Man shall not live by bread alone."* (Matt 4:4), He meant by this, that man should not live solely to nourish his body with bread and forget the nourishment of the soul. This is also clear when He said to His disciples: *"I have food to eat of which you do not know."* (John 4:32).

A question arises at this point:

Was Jesus, on the mount, fasting or being nourished?

The answer is that He was fasting and getting nourished at the same time. His body was fasting but His soul was being nourished.

His food was different too, of which the people knew nothing about. With nourishment for the soul, the body was supported for forty days and forty nights.

He teaches us that we should care for our spiritual and not bodily needs. In this we discover before our eyes the words of the Godly revelation as spoken by our teacher the Apostle Saint Paul when **he explained our attendance to the bodily and spiritual things.**

He says: "There is therefore now no condemnation to those who are in Christ Jesus, who do not walk according to the flesh, but according to the Spirit." (Rom 8:1). This is the way God wants us to follow when fasting and throughout our life.

The Apostle goes on to say: "For those who live according to the flesh set their minds on the things of the flesh, but those who live according to the Spirit, the things of the Spirit." (Rom 8:5).

Are you one who cares for spiritual or for the bodily things? Are you concerned with your spiritual progress or the welfare of your body, your spiritual health or that of your body? There is no doubt that if you attend to the health of your spirit the Lord will also grant you health to your body during the fasting period as previously explained.

The danger of caring for the body lies in the following hard statements:
"For to be carnally minded is death" and "Because the carnal mind is enmity against God." (Rom 8:6,7).

Who can comprehend these words and persist in accordance with the flesh?

The Apostle also says: "So then, those who are in the flesh cannot please God." (Rom 8:8).

Therefore, brethren, we are not indebted to the body that we may live according to it, *"For if you live according to the flesh you will die; but if by the Spirit you put to death the deeds of the body, you will live."* (Rom 8:13).

It is admirable the Apostle's saying, for in fasting we do not do away with the body but its evil deeds. We destroy the deeds of the body by the spirit that we may live. We do not torture the body but we rather do not submit to its deeds. We do not give the body its lusts and desires, but exaltation, loftiness above materialistic things, and the surrender to the Spirit, as the Apostle says: *"But to be spiritually minded is life and peace."* (Rom 8:6).

This is the meaning of fasting. Faced by the above statement of the Apostle, we ask:

Do you, in your fast, care for that what belongs to the Spirit?

This is what we would like to discuss in the following chapters so that our fast may be spiritual and acceptable before God. Not to concentrate on the bodily aspect of fasting and overlook the spiritual benefits. To comprehend the spiritual views of fasting and follow a spiritual route for our benefit.

If fasting is not bodily hunger but spiritual nourishment, then let us research what spiritual nourishment is and whether or not we achieve it while fasting.

CHAPTER THRÉE

CONSECRATE A FAST

✝ What is the meaning of the word ' Consecrate '?
✝ What is the aim of your fast?
✝ False and rejected fasts.
✝ What is the relationship between God and your fast?
✝ Lent.

The Lord said through the Prophet Joel: *"Consecrate a fast, Call a sacred assembly."* (Joel 1:14, 2:15).

What does it means to sanctify a fast? And how is it done?

The meaning of "Consecrate a fast"

The word "Consecrate" in its Greek origin means to sanctify. Thus when the Lord said to Moses: *"Consecrate to Me all the firstborn, whatever opens the womb ... it is Mine."* (Ex 13:2), He meant that those firstborn should be sanctified to Him and not for any other purpose. The firstborn males used to devote themselves to the service of the Lord before Aaron and his offspring. The firstborn of cattle were also offered as a sacrifice.

Sacred garments for the service of priests were consecrated to God. In this, the Lord said to Moses: *"So they shall make holy garments for Aaron your brother and his sons, that he may minister to Me as priest."* (Ex 28:4).

Altar vessels are sacred for the Lord, devoted to His service, and were not use for any other purpose. Sanctifying a house for the Lord is to devote it to Him and cannot be used for any other thing but the worship of the Lord: *"My house shall be called a house of prayer."* (Matt 21:13).

Some may ask: What does the Lord mean by His words to His disciples: *"And for their sakes I sanctify Myself."* (John 17:19). He means that He devotes Himself to them and the church for He came to redeem her.

Sacraments are the Lord's appropriations, they belong to the Lord alone and to no one else. They are consecrated to the Lord in the same way as the firstborn were. As the Lord says through the Prophet Ezekiel: *"There I will require your offerings and the firstfruits of your sacrifices, together with all your holy things."* (Ezek 20:40). About the first fruits of every fruitful tree, He says: *"But in the fourth year all its fruit shall be holy, a praise to the Lord."* (Lev 19:24). Their fruit was for the Lord and was given to the Lord's priests. (Ezek 44:30).

It was said that the money going into the Lord's money box in the sanctuary *"are consecrated to the Lord; they shall come into the treasury of the Lord."* (Josh 6:19) to be devoted to the Lord.

In the same way, days were consecrated or devoted to the Lord.

To "Remember the Sabbath day, to keep it holy." (Ex 20:8), to devote the day to the Lord, namely not performing any work for it is for the Lord. In the same way, we should consecrate to the Lord all His feast days on which holy gatherings are held, to cease from work and devote to the Lord. (Lev 23:3,7,8, 21,25,31,36).

Thus sanctification of fasting is to consecrate it to the Lord.

Days of fasting are sacred, and are devoted to the Lord. They do not belong to the world but to the Lord's as a sanctification to Him.

That is why God's inspiration clarified this meaning when He said *"Consecrate a fast, Call a sacred assembly"* (Joel 1:14,2:15), because a "sacred assembly" is fit for the consecration of the fast to the Lord, devoting it to Him.

However, what can you do if it is not possible for you to devote all your time to the Lord, and withdraw from your official work?

Withdraw as much as you can to devote yourself to God. However, if, despite your efforts, time becomes limited, devotion takes on another meaning:

At least, aim to devote the fast for the Lord.

In this way, it becomes a sacred fast, for it is consecrated to God as far as its aim and approach are concerned. In this we comprehend the dual meaning of the word sacred namely pure for it is to the Lord.

Is the Lord the aim of your fast?

Why do we fast? What is our goal when fasting? Our aims in fasting determine our means and according to our goal, results follow.

Do we fast merely because it is a rite, mentioned in the Kutamarus and the church calendar, or because the Church has announced it? If so, then internally we are not complete. Of course, obedience to the Church and the commandment is important, but obedience to the Commandment should be done in spiritual commitment and not in a superficial fashion. When the Church planned this fast, it did so for the sake of the spiritual depth that is in that fast.

So what is this spiritual depth? And what is the goal of our fasting? **Is it merely to deprive and humiliate the body?**

Deprivation of the body is in fact, not a virtue in itself but only a means by which the soul can take its hold. Do we therefore, confine ourselves to the means, or move to the target which is allows the soul to take its restrain?

How many are the false goals that rise before man in his fasts! **Some may fast merely for self-approval**, to feel pious, to gain approval in spiritual gatherings, to avoid being negligent to a biblical commandment or to gain praise from others for his fast or his level. In this way, one falls in to the sin of false self glory.

What then should be the sound aim in fasting?

Our aim should always be to fast out of love for God.

Out of love, we desire that our souls adhere to Him. We do not allow our bodies to hinder the way of the soul. Therefore, we subdue through fasting to make the body conform with the soul in its work. It is in fasting that we are likely to soar above the materialistic and bodily needs, and live by the soul. To allow the human soul to unite in God's Spirit in His work to enjoy His love and company.

Enjoying God's love and fellowship should be our manner throughout our lives. However, it should not be forgotten, that it is during our times of fasting that we deepen and strengthen our training and preparation for this enjoyment of God for other times of our life.

Thus, we fast because fasting brings us close to God.

Fasting in part, is a withdrawal which gives us an opportunity for prayer, spiritual reading, and contemplation. Fasting helps one keep vigilant, practice prostration and set the mood for prayer. Fasting is control over the will and a triumph over desires. This is the way to God to lead us to penitence and reconciliation with Him. When we fast we are nourished by *"Every word that proceeds from the mouth of God."* (Matt 4:4).

Therefore, we fast for the sake of God's love and fellowship. We fast because it helps us shun worldly and materialistic things and to make us ready for eternity and oneness with God.

If fasting is consecrated to God alone, and for the sake of His love, a question then arises:

Can a person fast but at the same time not consecrate his fast to God?

Yes, they are many who fast, but God has no share in. For instance, someone may fast while far from God. He fasts, yet he does not change, still in weaknesses. A person of high profile or authority may even fast as a customary act, lest he should be embarrassed or for the sake of his reputation. Another may fast purely for bodily reasons, while the soul has no part in his fast.

One may fast to parade his ascetic ability or skill to abstain from food. A person may abstain from food for a while and at the same time indulging in wordily lusts which he cannot abstain from!

Some think that fasting only is associated with food without God being a party to it. All their cares while fasting is; How long is the period of abstinence? When shall they eat? How can they lengthen the period of their abstinence? What will they eat? How can they keep themselves away from certain kinds of food? How can they fast for days? It appears as if fasting concerns two parties only: them and their food, or them and the body, without God being party to the fast in any way!! Is this a correct fast?!

57

Fasting is not a mere a bodily deed. Rather it is communion with God. A fast that does not have God in it is no fast at all.

We eat and we fast for God.

We eat for God so that our body may gain strength to serve God and perform our duties and responsibilities towards others. It is also for God that we hunger, to subdue the body lest it sin against God, to control and not be controlled bodily desires and lusts so that they may not control our actions. We behave in accordance with the spirit, not the body, for the sake of our love of God, and the fellowship with His Divine Spirit.

Fasting for any other reason, is rejected by God.

Erroneous and rejected fasts:

Not every fast is acceptable, and some are rejected by God. The Bible gives us examples of some of these rejected fasts.

1. **Fasting for self-praise.** It intentionally revealed and exposed for others to see and praise it. About this type of fast, the Lord said in His Sermon of the Mount, *"Moreover, when you fast, do not be like the hypocrites, with a sad countenance. For they disfigure their faces that they may appear to men to be fasting. Assuredly, I say to you, they have their reward. "But you, when you fast, anoint your head and wash your face, "so that you do not appear to men to be fasting, but to your Father who is in the secret place; and your Father who sees in secret will reward you openly."* (Matt 6:16-18).

   A fast to gain praise from others is not for God who has nothing to do with it. This it is a rejected fast.

2. **The proud Pharisee is another example of the unacceptable fast:**

The Pharisee stood before God flaunting his virtues and saying: "I fast twice a week; I give tithes of all that I possess." At the same time, he condemns the publican saying, "I am not like other men--robbers, evildoers, adulterers--or even like this tax collector." (Luke 18:9-14). That is why he did not leave the temple justified, as was the case of the broken-hearted tax collector.

This example shows us that unless fasting is accompanied with humility and a contrite heart , then it is rejected by God. For without humility fasting is out of self righteous and disdain for others. (Luke 18:9).

3. **A fast with a wrong aim is unacceptable.**

An example of this fast were the Jews who banded together "and bound themselves under an oath, saying that they would neither eat nor drink till they had killed Paul. Now there were more than forty who had formed this conspiracy" (Acts 23:12,13). Naturally, their fast was a sin. Moreover, we cannot call it a spiritual fast.

4. **The sinful fasts during the days of the Prophet Jeremiah:**

The Lord did not accept this fast and said to Jeremiah, "Do not pray for this people, for their good. "When they fast, I will not hear their cry; and when they offer burnt offering and grain offering, I will not accept them. But I will consume them."(Jer 14:11,12).

The Lord did not accept their fasts, prayers, and oblation because they lived an evil life and their hearts were not pure before Him.

Thus, fasting without repentance is unacceptable.

God wants a pure heart more than He does a hungry body.
A person's fast is invalid if his heart does not abstain from sins and his tongue from evil words. Even if he gives his body to be burned, it will not profit him. (1 Cor 13:3).

5. **Fasting without mercy and charity is unacceptable:**

The Lord explained this point to the Prophet Isaiah, saying: *"'Why have we fasted,' they say, 'and You have not seen? Why have we afflicted our souls, and You take no notice?' ... Indeed you fast for strife and debate ... Is it a fast that I have chosen, A day for a man to afflict his soul? ...Would you call this a fast, And an acceptable day to the Lord? "Is this not the fast that I have chosen: To loose the bonds of wickedness, To undo the heavy burdens, To let the oppressed go free, And that you break every yoke? Is it not to share your food with the hungry and to provide the poor wanderer with shelter--"* (Is 58:3-7).

A fast that does not go hand in hand with merciful deeds and a pure heart is unacceptable even if performed with humility and courtesy.

6. **Fasting that is not for God is invalid:**

Some may fast on doctor's orders. Another may fast to have a graceful body and good looks. Both fasts are not performed for God and or spiritual gain. A third person may go on a hunger strike and not for spiritual aim or for God's sake. A fourth may forsake food in distress or despair. Non of these fasts can be considered genuine. Again, we reiterate by saying that any fast which is not for God and spiritual gain, cannot be considered a fast and is not accepted by God.

What then, is an acceptable spiritual fast for God?

It is one where a profound relationship with God is established. It is a fast where you feel God in your life. It is a sacred period, which belongs to God and devoted entirety Him. It is a time when God's presence is very visible in your behaviour. It is a time with which your relationship with God increases and grows in a spiritual exultation which makes you long to stretch your fast and become endless.

This leads us to examine an important question:

What is the relationship between God and your fast?

What does God gain from your fast? What have you received from God? What were you able to sacrifice to God in your fast, and what blessings did He give you? Was your fast a sacred time in your life during which you experienced a spiritual revival allowing you to taste and observe how good God is? Did you experience a change in your behave in accordance with the soul and not with the flesh?

Fasting is not substituting one food for another, and is not abstaining from food for a certain period. All these are just means, but they do not constitute the essence of fasting of to free and exalt the soul from its bodily needs and above the influence of materialism. The soul and the body move in unity in loving God to enjoy His company. This is what is meant by a sacred fast, i.e. one devoted entirely to God.

You must devote three things: your heart, thoughts, and will in order to consecrate you fast to God.

You should not be overly occupied with food and drink. Rather, your abstention trains you to have a strong will over what you eat and drink. When you succeed in controlling what you eat, your will submits itself to God in all things and your desires will be **nothing but what God wants.**

This is the wisdom behind fasting. Controlling our desire for food extends itself to controlling our conduct, which displeases God. It is not sufficient to abstain from or eat vegetarian food while at the same time unable to control certain sins! You should strive to submit your will to God in all that you do, saying to Him, "Let it not be my will but yours."

Therefore, find out where your will departs from God's and concentrate on those areas in particular in order to present to God a virtuous willpower that will please Him.

Your training while fasting will stay with you after it, and it will be unlikely that you commit those sins again which you were able to control and shun while fasting. If you are unable, then what have you gained from your fast?

Make sure that fasting changes something in you.

Do not let a change of food be the only thing different you do in a fast. Let the fast be change towards a better life, a chance to remove the defects and weaknesses you feel exist in your relationship with God and people. What benefit otherwise would you have, if you subdued yourself during the fifty five days of Lent only to come out of it exactly as you had been before, without increasing your fellowship and communication with God?!

Think about the number of fasts that have passed by while you are still as you are, without change.

How many fasts have you kept up till now since you came to know God? How many years since you have passed observed the different fasts as well as the weekly Wednesdays and Fridays fasts?

If you had managed to overcome just one weak point for every fast you observed which reconciles you to God, you will have succeeded in tasting the sweetness of His will and the depth of your relationship with Him!

Do not pause at the formalities of fasting but delve into its depths.

Fasting is neither a mere set of formalities nor an ordinance or rite. Rather, it is a blessing given to us by God and organised by the Church for our spiritual benefit, to enlighten and train our souls of the idealism that we should follow for: *"Holiness, without which no one will see the Lord."* (Heb 12:14).

Fasting, therefore, is a sacred, idealistic, and extraordinary act. It requires a special spiritual planning to match its holiness. When a fast begins, we feel that we have entered a time of exultation and started extraordinary days of self training in living a life of perfection. Therefore, these days should not pass as other days do, for they constitute a new phase in our relationship with God - a phase that we go through with new feelings and spirit.

It is true that all the days of our life should be sacred. However, fasting days are more so than others. If we conduct ourselves well during these days, we shall attain the holiness for the rest of our life. It is a time when we devote ourselves, as much as we can, to God and deepen our relationship with Him.

Have you heard of the fast that exorcises evil spirits?

About these devils the Lord said: *"This kind does not go out except by prayer and fasting."* (Matt 17:21). What power is in these fasts that even the devils cannot stand but are exorcised? Is it mere abstention from food? Of course not. Rather, it is the strong relationship that binds the person who fasts with God and which the Devil cannot stand. It is the harmony between man and God, of love and spiritual relationship with God, which the Devil is deprived of. As soon as the Devil sees it, he grows weary and flees.

It is through fasting, that the man's heart clings to God which the devil cannot withstand, and escapes.

Does your heart cling to God while fasting?

Do you give Him your heart as you do with your will? Do you feel His love while you are fasting? Does this love clearly show in your prayers and contemplation while fasting? Have you ever forgotten about your food and drink, for the sake of His love?

Is it as if you say to your body while fasting: '"I have no time for you now. If you have or have not eaten it does not concern me. "Everything under the sky has its own time" and this is not your time. I am preoccupied with the spiritual work with God. Come join us if you want to have some substance in this fast. As for food, there is no room for it now. My food now is every word that proceeds out of the mouth of God."'

His feelings are the same as those of Saint John, saying: *"I was in the Spirit on the Lord's Day"* (Revelation 1:10).

There is no doubt that days of fasting belong to the Lord. Therefore, are you "in the spirit" during your fast? Have you utterly forgotten about your bodily needs, with all its desires and opted to live in the spirit during the fasting period? You are not indebted to your body except for the necessities without which it cannot survive. It is as if you were saying with the apostle Paul: *"Whether in the body or out of the body I do not know, God knows—"* (2 Cor 12:3).

Does God occupy your thoughts while you fast?

During the divine Mass the priest cries out saying: "where are your hearts?" and the congregation answers: "They are with the Lord." Likewise, I want to ask you the same question when you fast: "Where are your minds?" Can you answer, saying: "They are with the Lord?" is not a fast a sacred period devoted to God, and one during which thoughts must be occupied with God alone? Examine yourself, and determine if your thoughts wander during the fast.

Do worldly concerns fill your thoughts during a fast?

In the whirlwind of labour, news, and in conversation with others, you do not find time to give God your thoughts!

You may fast till sunset but your thoughts are not with God and your mind exhausted, roaming and conforming to the world! You may spend a lot of time in idle chat and trivial things and your thoughts are away from God. You may only remember Him only when you sit down to break your fast. Then, you pray before eating and mention to God the fact that you have been fasting. Is this the kind of spiritual fast that sets your conscience at ease?! Remember the words of the Prophet David: *"I have set the Lord always before me. "* (Ps 16:8).

He is there before me in every thing I do and in every word I say. He sees everything. I also set Him before me because He is my aim away from which I do not want to venture. He is before me and because of Him alone I fast. My fast is not to distract me from Him, but to have Him always before me.

If on regular days you remember all the time God before you, then how much more so should you be when fasting, a time devoted and consecrated to God?

If God is not in your thoughts, then you are not fasting.

A day of fasting which passes by without remembering God, should be crossed out of your fast, for it cannot be as included under the title: *"Declare a holy fast."* (Joel 1:14,2:15)...

Some may ask, how can I do this while living in the world and having many responsibilities that I must think about?

Keep a balance in accordance with three rules:

1. Do not let your responsibilities dominate in such a way as to take all your thoughts and not leave a place for God. Set limits to your responsibilities and allow the Lord His share.

2. Depart from any thought that does not please God, for such a thought does not coincide with the sacred scope of your life. As the Apostle Paul says: *"Bringing every thought into captivity to the obedience of Christ."* (2 Cor 10:5) Therefore, do not defile your fast with wrong thoughts, for any thoughts which please Christ should be kept while those which displease Him should be driven away.

3. Let God share in your thoughts and in your goals, and say:

It is for God's sake that I am pondering this topic.

It is good that you think about your responsibilities, but do not let them be separate from God's. It is God who has given them to you, and you think about them for His sake. Therefore, your thoughts about them should not be separate from God. It is for God that you think about the affairs of your business, about your lessons and studies, about your service, and about your family responsibilities, on the condition that your thoughts do not take you away from God who is the origin and the foundation of everything. Think about your responsibilities while saying to God:

Join in the work of Your faithful.

A student, for instance, may study while fasting and have God join him. He studies while God grants him the power to understand and to remember the information learnt in memory. This student says to God: "O Lord, I cannot understand all this by myself. You stay with me and make me understand and I shall thank you for it. I study, O Lord, neither for the sake of knowledge nor for my future, but for You so that all may know that Your children are successful, that they are faithful in all the deeds they undertake, and that the Lord is with them and assists them. Thus people give praise "

You say to God: It is for You that I eat, and for You that I fast.

It is for You that I eat to gain strength to stand up and pray, to sit up late and contemplate. To use for the service of Your children, and for others to know that Your children are faithful in their responsibilities.

I fast so that my soul comes to You, unhindered by my body. In this way, God will be with you in everything you do.

You also partake with Jesus Christ who fasted.

Join Him in fasting to the extent that your weak nature can stand. He fasted for you, therefore at least fast for yourself. He who rejected the wordily food, and you too partake with him in rejecting the perishing food. He, who is nourished by the love and companionship of His Father, likewise do the same. He, who gained victory over the devil whilst fasting, plead with Him to guide you to victory.

Fasting in this way, becomes nourishment for your spirit.

The most hazardous thing that exhausts those who fast is that neither the body nor the soul is nourished. Fasting becomes a period of deprivation and torture. This is not the intention of a spiritual fast. Moreover, deprivation of the body only, gives fasting a negative image while leaving out the positive nourishment of the soul.

Nourishment of the soul is: prayer, meditation, reading the Holy Bible, spiritual readings such as the sayings of Fathers and biographies of Saints, hymns and psalms, spiritual meetings and prostration etc.

Nourishment of the soul also includes spiritual feelings, God's love and all matters relating to eternity.

The soul that is nourished is able to support the body.

This is clearly seen during Passion Week when asceticism becomes intense, with long periods of abstinence. Nevertheless, the body endures without becoming tired because the soul is nourished by the memories of Christ's suffering by on Passion Week. Bible readings, hymns, and rites all focus the mind on Passion Week and the suffering of our Lord.

There are times when a person may be so absorbed by the satisfaction and pleasure of what he reads that he may forget about his craving for food so that he can proceed with his readings. The soul becomes nourished to the extent that it sustains the body, which does not feel any hunger.

Therefore, give the soul its nourishment during a fast and rest assured that nourishment of the soul gives the body the strength it needs to endure the fast. Moreover, fasting of the body empower the soul, for the spiritual action is intermingled with the bodily and mental asceticism. **Prayers and masses during a fast are more profound** during fasts for they emanate from a body, which has submitted to the soul. Your prayer becomes powerful since they emanate from a heart abstained from materialistic things and a soul abstained from the worldly lusts. Such as the vespers and midnight prayers performed with a light body abstaining from food.

During the fasts, our Fathers concerned themselves with the work of the soul. But what about their food?

Even while eating, they were also interested in nourishing their souls.

They used to take it in turn while they ate, to read aloud a Saint's biography or "Sayings of the Fathers". This helped withdraw their minds away from food and materialistic issues, and at the same time be nourished spiritually while they ate their food. They avoided being fully occupied with the body and became accustomed to the discipline of the soul over every bodily act.

The commandments oblige us to fast, but our Fathers did not fast because of them.

They fasted for the love and not for obedience to the commandment.

Obedience is for the novice, but love is for the mature and the perfect.

Our fathers fasted, not to fulfil a commandment, an imposition, or a rite, but for the spiritual pleasure in which they found spiritual satisfaction and comfort for their souls and bodies.

Our fathers did not stop fasting at the limits of obedience to the commandment, but they delved into its spirituality.

The spirituality of the commandment requires us to fast for our own good. Otherwise, God would not have ordered it.

In addition to what we have said, we shall, God willing, explain this matter in detail in the following chapter titled "The virtues that accompany fasting".

However, for now we shall talk about **Lent,** as the holiest fast of the year.

Lent comprises three fasts: the sacred forty days which Christ fasted, is preceded by a week considered either as an introductory week for the sacred forty days or as compensation for the Saturdays when abstention from food is not allowed. These are followed by Passion Week which constituted a separate fast independent of Lent at the to mark the beginning of the Apostolic era.

Lent is the holiest of all the annual fasts and its days are the holiest of all the days of the year. It correlates to Christ's fast and therefore very significant. The Church also considers it as a fast of the first degree.

It is a period of spiritual reserve up for the whole year.

He who does not benefit spiritually from it, will hardly benefit from the other less spiritual days. He who spends the days of Lent indifferently will find it hard to be particular about the rest of the year.

Try to benefit from this fast, its hymns, readings, rites, spirituality and the afternoon Masses

Our Fathers used Lent as an opportunity for preaching.

During this time people were more spiritual and were ready to accept it. Indeed, preaching is set for the whole year but the sermons of Lent have a more profound effect. That is why many of Saint John Chrysostom's books were sermons that he delivered during Lent. In the same way the books of Saint Augustine. Even the Church made these days of Lent a period for the preparation of those accepting the Faith.

It prepared them through preaching to accept the grace of baptism.

Classes for those new to the faith were held during the fast and sermons were delivered to teach and confirm them in the principles of Faith. They were then baptised on Christening Sunday, to join the faithful for the following week's Palm Sunday, in the Passion Week prayers, and in the Easter celebrations.

Saint Kirollos of Jerusalem for example, held sermons to prepare those attending to accept the Faith and explain to them the creed and the principle of faith on the days of Lent.

The Church considers Lent of such importance that it has laid for it special rites.

It has its own special tunes, longer period of abstention, special readings and responses, a special rite of burning the morning incense, and special prostration in the Mass before absolving the deacons.

During Lent, a special Katamarus of biblical readings is used and contains readings from the Old Testament to create a special spiritual atmosphere all of its own.

In order that faithful are prepared for the sacred forty days of Lent, the Church set the preparatory week so that people may not start the sacred period unprepared. It is also a way to make up for the Saturday when an abstinence period is allowed.

Furthermore, the Church established the fast of Jonah also in preparation for Lent.

The fast of Jonah or Nineveh occurs two weeks before Lent and has the same rite and tunes. It heralds the coming of Lent and prepares the congregation to repentance which is the essence of the fast of Nineveh.

In the same way that the Church has taken pains to prepare the its offspring for Lent. We should do our part by receiving it with the same concern.

If Jesus Christ observed this fast for us, though He did not need to, we should therefore fast it for ourselves since we are in great need of fasting to fulfil all righteousness, in the same way as Christ did.

The Church allocates so much importance to this fast that It calls it Lent which means the "Great" fast.

It is "Great" because of its duration and sanctity.

It is the longest of all fasts as it extents for fifty-five days, and it is the greatest in its sanctity as it is Christ's fast and commemorates His sacred suffering.

That is why a sin committed during Lent is most offensive.

It is true that a sin is a sin, but it is more horrible during Lent than during normal days because he who sins during any fast in general, and during Lent in particular, is actually committing a double sin. The offence of the sin itself and in addition the contempt shown for the holiness of those days. Therefore, they are two sins, not just one.

Carelessness for the sanctity of those days is indicative of the heart's cruelty, for a heart that is not affected by the spirituality of those sacred days is undoubtedly a cruel one from a spiritual point of view. He who sins during this fast is subject to the Lord Jesus Christ words who said: "If therefore the light that is in you is darkness, how great is that darkness!" (Matt 6:23).

If these sacred and inspiring days are a period of darkness, then how much more are the normal days ?

Saintly monks beheld the great Lent. Their whole lives were days of fasting, but the days of Lent were of special sanctity for the first generations of monks who used to leave the monasteries during the sacred forty days and live in isolation on the mountains. An example is found in the story of Saint Zosima and his encounter with the repentant Saint Mary the Copt.

The same zeal was found in the monasticism of Saint Shenoudah, chief of hermits, and in many of the Ethiopian monasteries.

Let us also be fervent during these sacred days.

If we are unable to fast the days in abstinence as did the Lord Jesus Christ, glory be to Him then at least let us try to be as serious and as pious as we can and to the limit of our endurance.

If we cannot reproach and forcefully defeat the Devil as did the Lord, at least let us be ready to resist him. Let us remember what the Apostle Saint Paul said in criticism to the Hebrews: "You have not yet resisted to bloodshed, striving against sin." (Heb 12:4).

Man should strive "to bloodshed " in resisting sin.

If the three days that Esther and her people fasted had their strong influence, how much more will the fifty five days in supplication to God?

At this point, I address all in reproach:

How many Lents have passed by us with all the spirituality's of the "Great Fast"? If we have gained some spiritual benefit from every fast, what is our harvest from these "Great Fasts" and from the other fasts that we kept?

The point is that, in fasting, we are in need of seriousness and spirituality and should not pursue the matter in a routine and careless manner.

CHAPTER FOUR

VIRTUES AND FEELINGS THAT ACCOMPANY FASTING

✞ Virtues accompany fasting
✞ Repentance.
✞ Prayer and worship.
✞ Self-abasement and penitence.
✞ Seclusion and silence.
✞ Fasting of the tongue, thought and heart.
✞ Self control.
✞ Conquering the body.
✞ Asceticism.
✞ Charity.
✞ Prostration.

Virtues accompany fasting

Those who fast and gain no benefit have done so in the wrong way. Fasting is not to blame but the method followed.

Such as those who fast bodily without paying attention to the virtues that accompany a fast. Or, those who's aim is fasting in itself as a the target although it should be a means towards an end, the means of giving the soul the opportunity.

Fasting is a period of intense spirituality, a period for loving God, and adhering to Him. This love for he who fasts helps elevate a person above body and its concerns. It a means of soaring above the worldly things to taste the heavenly matters. It is a period of sacred feelings towards God. At least it cultivates the feeling of closeness and communion with God. It is a period of spiritual struggle: with self, with God, and against the Devil.

The days of fasting are for spiritual strength and a period of storage.

From the depth of spiritual fast, one gains spiritual strength that sustains him during his period of no fasting. He who is honest for instance during Lent, stores up spiritual stock that strengthens him throughout the fifty sacred days following Lent, where neither fasting nor prostration are allowed

He who wants to fast in a spiritual manner, should keep the following points in mind:

1. **Fasting should be spiritual in aim and motive**
   It is not an obligation, for praise, or out of custom. We fast for the love of God above materialistic and bodily things, to give the soul a chance to grow.

2. **Fasting should be a period of penitence and purity of heart**:

   In it, a person leads a holy life, acceptable in the sight of God, confessing his sins, reproaches himself and then partakes of the Holy Sacraments.

3. **Fasting should be a period of spiritual nourishment accompanied by an effective spiritual agenda**:

   To use all the spiritual media available and to concentrate on spiritual rather than bodily matters. Not to focus on the type of vegetable food to be eating but on the sanctity of these days of fasting and what is proper for them so that one's spirit may be strengthened

Fasting leads to the strength of the spirit, and the strength of the spirit leads to fasting.

Virtues which are intermingled, are gained through fasting

Fasting helps one stay up late because of the lightness of one's body. Staying up late leads to reading and prayer. Spiritual reading also helps one to pray. Spiritual work as a whole makes a spiritual person sit up late. Reading is a source of contemplation. Contemplation strengthens prayer which is also a source of contemplation.

Fasting is associated with prostration, which leads to humility and a contrite heart. A subdued body through fasting also leads to a subduing of the soul.

Fasting leads to virtues, which relate to the purpose of fasting.

The Apostles for example, prepares one for service. Nineveh's fast, aims at repentance. The purpose of a fast, such as Esther's, was to save her people. There are those who fast for others and their fast embodies love, sacrifice, and cooperation. These are all fasts, which relates to with special virtues.

We should remember in our fast that the Lord Jesus Christ fasted while He was filled with the Spirit. As for us let at least fast so that we may become filled with the Spirit.

Fasting accompanies repentance:

Days of fasting days are sacred and man lives them in holiness.

During these days, the mind, heart and body must also be sacred. Fasting is a period of training during which you attempt to approach God and at the same time, sin pulls you away. Therefore, you must eliminate sin through repentance to draw close to God.

While fasting, your body abstains from food, and your soul abstains from every earthly and worldly lust, and all passions that pertain to the body. Through repentance therefore, you approach God. Ask yourself, are you fasting this way?

Without repentance, God rejects and does not accept your fast. You do not gain either heaven or earth and you torment yourself in vain. If you want God to accept your fast, examine your sins, and revoke them. God gave us as a symbol a lesson when He accepted the baptism of repentance before he fasted.

Take the example of the fast of Nineveh:

The Bible says about the people of Nineveh that *"every one turn from his evil way and from the violence that is in his hands."* (Jon 3:8). For this reason, God did not destroy them when He *"saw their works, that they turned from their evil way."* (Jon 3:10). The bible did not say: "when He saw their as sackcloth or their fast," but when he saw their repentance which was the principal element of their fast.

In the Book of Joel, we see an example of repentance that accompanies fasting.

The Lord addresses the people through His prophet saying: *"Turn to Me with all your heart, With fasting, with weeping, and with mourning." So rend your heart, and not your garments; Return to the Lord your God, For He is gracious and merciful. "* (Joel 2:12,13). It is clear that fasting was accompanied by repentance and weeping. Therefore, it is not mere abstention from food. Rather, it is inner emotions towards God.

In his fast, the Prophet Daniel offered the repentance of the whole nation.

He fasted, confessing to God, saying: *"We have sinned and committed iniquity, we have done wickedly and rebelled, even by departing from Your precepts and Your judgments. ... O Lord, righteousness belongs to You, but to us shame of face ... O Lord, to us belongs shame of face, to our kings, our princes, and our fathers, because we have sinned against You."* (Dan 9:5-8).

We therefore reconcile with God through fasting.

Do not say: "How long, O Lord? Will You forget me forever? (Ps 13:1). You should rather say: 'How long will I forget You, O Lord, forever? How long will I hide my face from You?

Therefore purify and sanctify your soul. Prepare for these special days. Make ready to have God residing in your hearts and not by merely abstain from food.

If you are in sin, be reconciled with God, and if you are reconciled with Him, deepen your love for Him.

If you removed sinfulness in a fast, continue in the same way afterwards.

Repentance is not confined to fasting alone, but made fit through fasting. Through fasting, man heart is purified, and this purity continues with him.

In all this, be ready to strive against the Devil.

Joshua, son of Sirakh, told his son that if he set forward to serve God, he should prepare himself for all trials.

When the Devil sees your fast and repentance, he becomes envious of your spiritual acts. Thus, he fights you to deprive you of the fruit of your labour and seeks every trick to bring about your downfall, saying: I shall not leave you until you give up. Remember the words of the Apostle Peter, who said, *"Resist him, steadfast in the faith. "* (1 Pet 5:9).

Thus, fasting is a period of spiritual warfare as was the case with Jesus Christ. (Matt 4). It is also a period of triumph for him who shares it with Christ.

Fasting accompanies prayer and worship:

Fasting without prayer is a bodily act. As such, it loses its spiritual nature and benefit.

Fasting does not mean depriving the body of food, which is a negative aspect. The positive aspect manifests itself in giving the soul its nourishment.

Those who fast without any spiritual act, such as prayer, contemplation, spiritual reading, Psalms, Hymns, or prostration, their fast becomes a useless burden. What is the difference between their fast and that of the Buddhists and Hindus? What role did the Holy Spirit play in your fast?

Fasting provides an opportunity for prayer. A prayer while fasting is more profound than one hundred prayers conducted with a full stomach full and a voice jolting mountains.

The Church teaches us that prayer and fasting are interrelated. In the Lent Fraction during the divine Mass, the statement "Through prayer and fasting" is repeated a number of times. When the Lord Jesus Christ spoke about exorcising devils, He said: *"This kind does not go out except by prayer and fasting."* (Matt 17:21).

Well-known fasts in the Bible were also bound to prayer.

Thus, when Nehemiah fasted, he said: "When I heard these words, that I sat down and wept, and mourned … And I said: "I pray, Lord God of heaven, … let Your ear be attentive and Your eyes open, that You may hear the prayer of Your servant which I pray before You now, day and night… " (Neh. 1:4-6). He then started confessing his sins and the sins of his people calling for the Lord's intervention and mercy.

Ezra's fast was also accompanied by prayers. (Ezra 8:21,23).

The Prophet Daniel's fast was accompanied by prayer and struggle with God. He said, "O my God, incline Your ear and hear; open Your eyes and see our desolations, and the city which is called by Your name; for we do not present our supplications before You because of our righteous deeds, but because of Your great mercies. "O Lord, hear! O Lord, forgive! O Lord, listen and act! Do not delay for Your own sake, my God, for Your city and Your people are called by Your name." (Dan 9:18,19).

In the fast of Nineveh, the people cried *"mightily to God"* (Jon 3:8).

Therefore, cry to God during your fast, lifting up your abased heart to Him.

Be confident that God will respond to your fast and clamour, and that when He reproaches the winds and the waves, the sea will become calm. How deep indeed are your prayers if conducted on sacred days from a humbled hearts before God through fasting and purified by repentance. How much more profound they become if accompanied by attendance to the Holy Mass and communion.

Train yourself while fasting in the love of prayer and the struggle with God.

In Chapter five, we have written out a up a guide for your prayer.

It is important in prayer, to submit your heart and thought to God.

Do not subdue your conscience with formalities and with

shallow readings not emanating from the heart, and then say: " I have fasted and prayed!" God will blame you, saying: "This people honours Me with their lips, But their heart is far from Me." (Mark 7:6). Prayer is a fellowship, thus, during your prayer and fasting feel that you are in communion with God.

If consecrating a fasting means devoting it to God, then have you devoted your fasting period to prayer and spiritual work?

Is it a period of prayer, contemplation, spiritual storage, and devotion to God and His company? Are your prayers double or triple those of your regular days? If you have not devoted most of your time to God, have you devoted your feelings and emotions to Him?

Fasting, accompanied by an intimate relationship with God, becomes spiritual enjoyment.

In this kind of enjoyment, one tries to increase his fasts and his food becomes heavy for him because causes him to use his body which took some rest during the hours of abstention.

Fasting is accompanied by self-abasement and weeping:

Fasting is a period for an abased soul before God through repentance, tears and humility. Thus one becomes aware of its weakness, knows that he is form dust and ashes and appeals to the Higher Power.

When the body is humbled by hunger, the soul too is humbled. Thus, it humbles itself while it bows down before God in obedience and humility confessing its sins. Humility softens the heart of God and all the dwellers of Heaven.

In his humility and weakness, man renounces all. His heart is no longer attached to any wordily lusts and he addresses God in a profound manner.

The Holy Bible presents us with several examples of self-abasement in fasting since God cannot bear to see the humility of His children before Him. Examples abound in the Book of Judges where God saw the humility of His people, descended, and saved them. (Judges 2). *"In all their affliction He was afflicted, And the Angel of His Presence saved them."* (Is 63:9).

Through self-abasement and defeat, the people become humble and the Lord comes need those who are humbled and to those with a crushed heart and He saves them.

The fast that the Prophet Joel ordered is a clear example: He said: *"Gird yourselves and lament, you priests; ... Come, lie all night in sackcloth, You who minister to my God; ... Consecrate a fast, Call a sacred assembly. "* (Joel 1:13,14) *"Now, therefore," says the Lord, "Turn to Me with all your heart, ... Consecrate a fast, Call a sacred assembly ... Let the bridegroom go out from his chamber, And the bride from her dressing room. Let the priests, who minister to the Lord, Weep between the porch and the altar; Let them say, "Spare Your people, O Lord, And do not give Your heritage to reproach, That the nations should rule over them. Why should they say among the peoples, 'Where is their God?' "* (Joel 2:12-17).

Here we see details of a integral fast.

Fasting, together with repentance (returning to God), prayer, self abasement, weeping, lamentation, shunning bodily desires, seclusion are all elements of fasting and no longer becomes mere abstention from food.

Another example is the fast of the people of Nineveh.

All the people, even children and babies, fasted and neither ate nor drank anything. They did not stop at that but humbled themselves before God, covering themselves with sackcloth and ashes. Even the King himself removed his crown and royal attire, did not sit on his throne but sat with the people on sackcloth and in ashes and they all cried mightily unto God. (Jon 3).

Such also was the fast of Nehemiah and that of Ezra.

Ezra, the scribe and priest, said: *"Then I proclaimed a fast there at the river of Ahava, that we might humble ourselves before our God, to seek from Him the right way for us and our little ones ... So we fasted and entreated our God for this, and He answered our prayer."* (Ezra 8:21,23).

Nehemiah also said: "I sat down and wept, and mourned for many days; I was fasting and praying before the God of heaven." (Neh 1:4). He said this about himself, but as for the people, he said that they "were assembled with fasting, in sackcloth, and with dust on their heads. Then those of Israelite lineage separated themselves from all foreigners; and they stood and confessed their sins and the iniquities of their fathers. And they stood up in their place and read from the Book of the Law of the Lord their God for one-fourth of the day; and for another fourth they confessed and worshiped the Lord their God." (Neh 9:1-3). Is this not also an integrated fast: through prayer, weeping, lamentation, Bible reading, repentance, confession, and abasing oneself in sackcloth and ash! Therefore, fasting is not merely abstention from food.

In the same way was the Prophet Daniel's fast.

He said: "Then I set my face toward the Lord God to make request by prayer and supplications, with fasting, sackcloth, and ashes. And I prayed to the Lord my God, and made confession … "we have sinned and committed iniquity, we have done wickedly and rebelled, even by departing from Your precepts …" (Dan 9:3-5).

In another fast, he says: *"I, Daniel, was mourning three full weeks. I ate no pleasant food, no meat or wine came into my mouth, nor did I anoint myself ... "* (Dan 10:2,3). This fast constitutes the same elements as the previous fasts.

This is indeed the fast that the Prophet David referred to, saying: *"My clothing was sackcloth; I humbled myself with fasting "* (Ps 35:13).

There is no doubt that lamentation constrains the bodily lusts and removes all desire for food. Moreover, humility opens the gates of Heaven.

Fasting accompanies seclusion and stillness:

The following statement was repeated twice in the book of the Prophet Joel: "Consecrate a fast, Call a sacred assembly." (Joel 1:14,2:15).

Call a sacred assembly, namely "retire", so that you may find time for spiritual nourishment.

In seclusion, you keep silent, and since you have no one to talk to, you talk to God. However, do not remain secluded in sin or in vain thoughts, but do so in order that your fast may not become visible to anyone except to your Father in Heaven who sees in secret. Moreover, one who fasts may be in such a state of asceticism, hunger, and weakness that one is unable to make any effort. Seclusion is therefore more suitable for him.

When a person fasts, his soul is occupied with internal work with God. Speaking hinders one's prayer, preoccupation and contemplation. Meetings and visitations hinder one's devotion to God and may lead one into making mistakes.

In fasting, the Lord Jesus Christ retired to the mountain, in seclusion with God, the Father, and devoted Himself to contemplation.

Our Fathers' fasted in the same way in the wilderness. As for you, retire as best as you can, and if you are forced to mingle, do it within the limits of necessity. Rid yourself of lost time and of every trivial word.

This brings to mind another fast which is:

Fasting of the tongue, thought, and heart:

Saint Isaac said: "the fasting of the tongue is better than the mouth's, and the abstinence of the heart from lust is better than both fasts" this shows the importance of fasting of both the tongue and the mouth.

Many concern themselves with abstaining from food. God rebuked them, saying: *"Not what goes into the mouth defiles a man; but what comes out of the mouth, this defiles a man."* (Matt 15:11). In this way He shows us that wrong words are defiling. In the same way, our teacher, the Apostle James, refers to the tongue which "defiles the whole body." (James 3:6). Is your tongue, thus, fasting with the rest of your body? And is your heart abstaining from lusts?

A fasting heart is able to make the tongue fast with it, for *"out of the abundance of the heart the mouth speaks."* (Matt 12:34).

The Lord also said, "But those things which proceed out of the mouth come from the heart, and they defile a man. " (Matt 15:18). Moreover, "A good man out of the good treasure of his heart brings forth good things, and an evil man out of the evil treasure brings forth evil things." (Matt 12:35). Therefore, if your heart abstains from sin, your tongue will abstain from every evil word.

He who fasts the heart, can also make his body fast also.

Therefore, what is important is for the heart and thought to abstain from every wrong desire assisted by the fasting of the body, which is the least of all. Therefore in your fast, control your tongue and in the same way that you make your mouth refrain from food, make it refrain from bad words. Control your thoughts and yourself.

Fasting accompanies self-control:

It is commendable that you control yourself against every wrong desire whether it comes to you from your inside or from warring devils, for *"he who rules his spirit"* is better than *"he who takes a city."* (Prov 16:32).

Therefore, hold the reins of self-control in your hand.

In a bodily fast, your body longs for food. You say: No, and you succeed in applying this "No". Make therefore, this willpower include every thought, every wicked desire, every wrong behaviour, and every bodily lust.

As for the person who only controls his food and is controlled by his lusts, his fast is a bodily one. He who cannot control his bodily fast is consequently unable to control himself from bad thought, lusts, and conduct.

Control of your lusts is proof of your asceticism and love of God.

Vanquishing the body:

While fasting, say to the body: "Let go of the soul and release it from your bonds that it may delight in God. You fast that your soul may be released from the bonds of the body. Desire for food is one of these bonds. These are also other ties such as bodily lusts.

Defeating the body through fasting, is also accomplished by staying away from marital relationships, provided it is done "with consent." (1 Cor 7:5). As the Prophet Joel says about fasting, *"Let the bridegroom go out from his chamber, And the bride from her dressing room."* (Joel 2:16), and as was said about king Darius when he cast Daniel into the den, he *"spent the night fasting; and no musicians were brought before him."* (Dan 6:18).

Even the mere adornment of the body was referred to by the Prophet Daniel in his fast. He said: *"nor did I anoint myself at all"* and *"till three whole weeks were fulfilled."* and *"I ate no pleasant food."* (Dan 10:3).

Vanquishing the body is not an aim in itself but rather a vehicle for the soul.

Vanquishing the body is necessary lest it should digress and lead to the destruction of the soul. On this matter, the apostle says in earnest, *"But I discipline my body and bring it into subjection, lest, when I have preached to others, I myself should become disqualified."* (1 Cor 9:27). When the body is vanquished, the soul takes control and the body not resisting, but collaborating with it and submitting to its leadership.

Therefore, control your body and keep it wisely from all futile enjoyment, luxury, and lust.

It is not enough that you fast, for you also need to overcome the lust for food.

This leads us to asceticism in fasting as another virtue.

Asceticism:

Man may abstain from food but craves it. Therefore there is no gain in abstinence from food but in renouncing it.

Rising above the level of eating leads one to abstinence from and letting go of food. In turn, this leads to the virtue of detachment. Nevertheless, what should you do if you cannot accomplish renunciation and detachment?

If you cannot achieve renunciation and detachment, then at least give up something for the sake of God.

Adam and Eve were required to keep away from one fruit. It was not an issue of abstinence from food or one item of it but a sort of training to renounce everything for God's sake...

As for you when you fast, what can you renounce for God's

sake, for His love and for the preservation of His commandments?

God is not is need of your renunciation of anything. However, by doing this, you show your love for God in profound and practical way, and for the sake of His love, you sacrificed your desires.

Fasting accompanies charity:

He who hungers while fasting sympathises with the hungry. For this mercy, God accepts his fast as He said, *"Blessed are the merciful, For they shall obtain mercy."* (Matt 5:7). Out of its concern for charity, the Church chants the hymn of "Blessed are those who show mercy to the needy" during Lent.

Out of His concern for charity, the Lord said in Isaiah's prophecy: "Is this not the fast that I have chosen: To loose the bonds of wickedness ... To let the oppressed go free ... Is it not to share your bread with the hungry, And that you bring to your house the poor who are cast out; When you see the naked, that you cover him, And not hide yourself from your own flesh?" (Is 58:6, 7).

During the age of martyrs and confessors, the Church used to preach that:

If you have nothing to give to those in need, then fast and offer them your food.

Do not fast to save food for yourself, but rather that you fast and give the food you saved to the needy. It has been the custom for many churches during the days of fasting to hold banquets for the poor so as not to embarrass the poor by having them eat all by themselves, the whole congregation eat together.

Fasting is accompanied by prostration:

Prostration is in fact a series of successive prostration accompanied by short prayers.

The Church combines prostration with abstinence from food for a number of hours. Thus, on days when abstinence is not allowed, - e.g. feast days, Saturdays, Sundays, and the fifty days following Easter – then prostration are also not permissible. A belly full of food is not fit spiritually or bodily for prostration. Prostration are therefore better observed in the early morning or at any time during fasting before food is eaten.

Prostration may be a form of self-abasement before God.

Every prostration, man rebukes himself before God for on of his sins and asks for forgiveness, saying: I have sinned, O Lord, in doing this or that, so please forgive me. I have desecrated Your temple, so please forgive me. Forgive me, for I am lazy, negligent.... etc.

Prostration may be accompanied by prayers of gratitude and praise.

Spiritual preliminaries, such as self-examination or any spiritual reading to soften the heart, may precede prostration.

✤ ✤ ✤

CHAPTER FIVE

DRILLS WHILE FASTING

What are these drills?
- ✟ Drills pertaining to fasting.
- ✟ Drills pertaining to repentance.
- ✟ Seclusion and silence drills.
- ✟ Resisting lost time drills.
- ✟ Penitence and self-abasement drills.
- ✟ Memorisation drills.
- ✟ Prayer drills.
- ✟ Other spiritual media drills.
- ✟ Drills in certain virtues

What are these drills?

Since the fasting period is a sacred spiritual, during which one aims to develop spiritually, it is proper that one should place before him, some spiritual drills to convert these spiritual desires into a practical mode of living. So, what are these drills?

Spiritual drills vary from one person to another according to their requirements. These drills may include things like resisting some weak facets in the life of a fasting person, gaining certain virtues that such a person lacks, or spiritual longings pervading his heart.

Thus, they differ in the same person in accordance with his needs.

A person's needs will differ from time to time in accordance with his struggles on the one hand and his degree of development on the other hand.

What is important is set up spiritual drills so that the person who fasts may feel that he has before him a certain target against which he will examine himself and which he will pursues to accomplish clear result in addition to the general virtues of fasting that are of benefit to him.

What we are going to discuss now is by way of example.

Every person should set whatever exercises are appropriate to him in his fast provided that this is done, as much as possible, under the supervision of his Confession Father.

1. **Drills pertaining to fasting:**
   The purpose of these drills is to pursue a sound and developing fast.

Some of these drills pertain to self-control.

They may include stopping oneself from eating certain kinds of food that one covets. This may mean a total stop throughout the fasting period, a partial stop during a limited period or on a certain day, a reduction of the quantity of the food, or abstinence from a certain item of food.

Self-control drills may include the length of abstinence, its conditions and self-development during such a period. Some people resort to a system of gradual progression even within one fast. Lent for example, covers eight weeks during which one may gradually advance in degree of his asceticism and abstention from food.

Self-control also includes eating in moderation before beginning of a fast and on feast days. Eating on these days should not be gluttonous and uncontrolled. Self-control also includes the element of hunger.

Drills may embrace virtues accompanying fasting.

In this way they include the spiritual aspects of fasting such as self-control in areas outside the scope of eating such as control of the body, abstention from bodily lusts and all sensuous luxuries, spiritual vigils and keeping away from luxuries.

There are also drills that pertain to what fasting including humiliation and penitence before God and gradual growth in asceticism.

2. Drills pertaining to repentance:

Since fasting is a period of repentance, and repentance drills are numerous, let me mention the following:

(a) Concentration on a point of weakness or a favourite sin:

Each person knows perfectly well which sin he easily falls into and which sin he repeatedly commits and repeatedly referred to in his confessions. Try to discard on of these sins while fasting. In this way, your fast indeed becomes sacred.

(b) Train yourself to quit a certain habit while fasting.

An example of this is a smoker who trains himself while fasting to quit smoking. Likewise he who is addicted to drinking coffee or tea and cannot rid himself of this habit. Likewise the person who is addicted by to watching television, wasting his time, discharging himself of his responsibilities.

The period of fasting is an opportunity for to all of them to quit their habits.

(c) Fasting could be a period of quitting a sin of anger or judgement of others.

Many people fall into this well-known sin. Drills may deal with eliminating a number of verbal sins that one may have become accustomed to saying. In fasting, he may train himself in elimination them one by one.

(d) How easy it is for man to condemn his sinful actions by using verses from the bible:

For instance, if he slips into the sin of anger, he reminds himself of the Bible verse: *"For the wrath of man does not produce the righteousness of God."* (James 1:20). He should repeat this verse often every day especially in situations where anger wars upon him. He should rebuke himself saying: What benefit is my fast if I anger and do not do the will of God?

If he slips into any of the spoken sins, he puts the following words of the Bible before his eyes: *"Every idle word men may speak, they will give account of it in the day of judgment."* (Matt 12:36). He then says to himself in reproach: To what benefit is my fast in self-control but can not control my tongue saying to my brother: *"You fool"* thus deserving of *"hell fire?"* (Matt 5:22).

(e) Whenever you feel hungry and covet food, rebuke yourself:

Say to yourself: When you give up this sin, I shall allow you to eat, for the Bible says: "If anyone will not work, neither shall he eat." (2 Thess 3:10), and you have not repented in a way befitting the fast or befitting a heart that is the residence of God.

Rebuke yourself, and say to it: What is the use of me shunning food if I have not yet given up the sin that separates me from God and that makes all my fast of no avail?

(f) Take your point of weakness and make it the topic of your prayers and the target of your efforts during your fast.

Concentrate fully to be careful and exacting and in resisting it.

Pour yourself before God, and say to Him: Save me, O'Lord, from this sin. I admit my weakness in this particular case and will not conquer it without Your help. Have mercy, O'Lord, on my weakness and helplessness. I do not want to conclude this fast before this sin is eradicated from my life.

Collect Bible verses that deal with this sin. Place them before you so that you may read them constantly.

Let fasting be a period of struggle with God so that he may grant you fortitude to conquer your sins. Train yourself while fasting in this kind of struggle, and say: Since, according to the Lord's words, fasting exorcises the evil ones, may it exorcise the devils that wars within me with the sins with which I am weak. May it exorcise my sins as it exorcised devils when coupled with prayer.

3. Solitude and silence drills

The Bible states: *"Consecrate a fast, Call a sacred assembly."* (Joel 1:14). Place this verse before you and train yourself in solitude.

What is meant by solitude is being in seclusion with God, for there are those who isolate themselves at home doing in no spiritual work and concentrate on the radio, television, or magazines, or delve into conversation with others at home! Or they may indulge in sinful thoughts!

Seclusion should actually be indulgence in spiritual work that you do with your bedroom door closed between you and God.

You seclude yourself with the Bible, with the biographies of saints, with prostration, and with prayer.

If you have a spiritual agenda you will love seclusion.

If you benefit by your seclusion in a spiritual way, you will pursue it and feel that it is a blessing from God.

Therefore, set a schedule, devote yourself to implement it. Try to free yourself during this period from your friends and recreations, for God will become your true friend in this period, and train yourself to do without useless talk and idle chatter. You will then be able to seclude yourself and labour with God.

If you cannot be in seclusion throughout the fast, then try the following:

Use the drill of "Some closed days."

This means that you specify certain days during which you do not leave home. You should organise your business, concerns and visits in such a way as to enable you to seclude yourself on these closed days. You may begin with one day a week, then two, then more.

However, what should you do if you cannot seclude yourself with God?

If you cannot close your doors during a fast, then at least secure your mouth against sinful words.

How easy it is for our conversation with people to hamper our discourse with God. As one of the Fathers said: "He who talks much is empty from the inside and is void of neither prayer, contemplation, nor spiritual recitations or spiritual work inside the heart.

Training in seclusion and retreat helps you remain silent, and silence rids you of the spoken mistakes and gives you the opportunity for internal growth which is the work of the soul.

Nevertheless, what full seclusion is not possible, what then?

There is another drill, which is:

4. Avoiding lost time:

There are one who wastes time. To him, time is trivial, wasted without benefit. This is his primary sin. He thus, neither prays, reads, nor has any spiritual contemplation. Consequently, spiritual laxity, and perhaps slipping into sin may ensue.

Such a person may say to himself: While fasting, I want to train myself to resist wasting my time and to make use of it. How can this be done?

Salvage the time lost in talking with people, in meetings, visitations, in useless discussions and in reading magazines and newspapers and expressing your view on their contents. The time wasted in listening in to the radio, watching television, and doing other dispensable and recreational things, should be used to do spiritual work for God.

We all know how we waste time, and therefore can best determine how best to save it as an integral part of his life. Let this then train ourselves on this point while we fast, God willing.

This drill helps us another way in **fasting of the tongue.**

Saint Isaac said that to fast the tongue is better than to fast the mouth. If you realise this, you will train yourself to remain silent as long as you can. If you are unable to do so, then use the following three exercises:

(a) Do not initiate a conversation except when necessary.

(b) Give short answers.

(c) Occupy your mind with some spiritual thought that will help you keep silent.

5. Penitence and self-abasement drills:

Fasting days are ones of penitence and self-abasement before God. Therefore, train yourself in them until you humble yourself down to the level of dust and ashes. This can be accomplished through the following exercises:

(a) Shun the love of praise, boastful talk, and self praise.

(b) Use penitent words in your prayers. For instance, repeat the words of the Psalm: *"O Lord, do not rebuke me in Your anger, Nor chasten me in Your hot displeasure."* (Ps 6:1).

(c) If you feel hungry or sit down to eat, say to yourself: "I do not deserve this food because of my sins, because I have done so and so. I do not fast out of holiness but out of my internal humility." He who attains penitence feels no desire for food no matter how appetising it is when laid before him. If hunger presses on him, he says to himself: "Repent first, then eat." If he still finds himself fallen into sin, he scolds himself, saying: "Is this a fast acceptable to God? Does this sanctify my fast?"

(d) Days of fasting are a good opportunity for confession and self-reproach inside oneself before God and before your Father confessor.

It is a period to be honest with oneself, holding yourself accountable and for rebuke and discipline. Remember not to justify yourself by finding excuses however trivial these may be.

(e) Train yourself in labour of humility which are numerous and about which we shall write a book for you, God willing.

6. Memorisation drills:

You may also take the period of fasting as a time for biblical verse memorisation of Psalms, chapters from the Bible, and church melodies and hymns.

(a) Take for instance the memorisation of the 111 verses of the Sermon on Mount. If you memorise three verses a day, you will finish with them in 37 days.

(B) Memorise for example, the passages of the prayers of the Agbia hours that are 36 in number. If you memorise one passage a day you will complete them in 36 days.

(c) Memorise the 8 hourly absolutions, as well as the

common prayers like the Introductory prayer, thanksgiving prayer, psalm 50 and concluding prayer, as well as some passages that are unique in the morning or the evening prayers.

(d) Memorise as many of the hourly psalms as you can, beginning with the short ones.

(e) Memorise selected Bible verses, preferably with their references. If you memorise three verses a day, you will have managed to memorise 150 new verses every year during Lent alone.

(f) You can memorise verses that begin with the letters of the alphabet. You may also memorise verses that carry certain meanings, or refer to the Church Sacraments or to certain parts of the creed, or those relating to every virtue.

(g) During a fast, you may memorise well known chapter of the Holy Bible such as (1 Cor 13), which is devoted to love; (Rom 12), which is a set of golden verses referring to several virtues; (1 Thess 5:12-23); (Eph 6:10-18) which are devoted to spiritual warfare and struggle (Phil 3:7-14), and the like from selected Bible chapters.

(h) Use the verses you memorised for spiritual meditation and nourishment during your fast and use them for practical application.

(i) Always recite the prayers and Psalms you have memorised in order to add them to your daily prayers.

(j) In the same way, set yourself a schedule for the memorisation of Church melodies and hymns.

Setting up a spiritual schedule, will make you realise the

importance and value of this time of fasting, and will therefore treasure for use to your benefit.

7. Prayer drills:

Make it your aim throughout the days of fasting to increase your prayer. Do not fall short in your Agbia or your normal prayers. We place before you, the following drills which your should try to perform to the best of your ability.

(1) Prayer drill while travelling:

While on your way, use the psalms, short or special prayers to occupy and lift up your heart to God. You may say:

Forgive me my God and do not take my sins into account. Have mercy on me, You the all merciful God. Save me, O'Lord, from my weaknesses and strengthen me. Bless O'Lord these sacred days, and bless these days of fasting. Allow me, O'Lord, to spend a period of time with Your. Unite my heart to You, O'Lord and fill me with love. Grant me your blessings, O'Lord and assist me. Bestow upon me a blessed and a pure heart. Wash me, and make me whiter than snow. Purify me and save me O'Lord. Protect me from all evil. Partake in this work with me. Let it be according to Your mercy and not according to my sins.

Train yourself in these and other similar types of prayers while on the road travelling. What is important is to keep your heart occupied always with God.

(2) Train yourself to pray in the midst of others:

Whether you are in a meeting, with friends or relations, or in the midst of people anywhere, lift up your heart in silence to God. In this way, you keep quiet while your heart is busy conversing with the Holy Spirit. For a silent person is a store of God's secrets. As the Spiritual man says, "Silence your tongue so that your heart may speak".

(3) Learn to pray while working:

Manual labour can easily be intermingled with prayer. It was thus with our forefathers, but may be different to the work performed by people living in the world. Even if your work requires mental concentration, try to lift up your heart to God from time to time with a very short prayer, saying: "I long for You, O'Lord. I do not want to stay for long away from You. Make me work be dedicated for You. Bless all that I do. I love You, O Lord from all my heart and I long for You. I praise Your Holy Name while I work. Your Name is sweet and blessed in the mouths of Your saints. I thank You, O'Lord, from all my heart. Be with me. Collaborate with me in my work. Do not let work detach me from my fellowship with You. Nothing takes me away from loving Jesus Christ.

(4) Train yourself in contemplation during prayer:

Take for example, the prayers of the psalms and the hourly Agbia prayers as a mean for spiritual contemplation. When you pray in this way by reciting them, you do so profoundly. Do the same with the Mass prayers and the church hymns so that they may influence your heart when you hear them.

(5) Train yourself to remain in pray:

Train yourself to prolong your prayer whenever you find that prayer is about to come to an end, even for two minutes longer. It is important is that you do not hasten to conclude it and leave the presence of God. Resist and continue even for a very short time. Then take your permission from God and end your prayer.

(6) Practice purity and spirituality in prayer:

These drills are numerous. They include prayers performed with understanding, depth, warmth, humility, and penitence as well as without folly and distraction. If you are unable, then carry out the following drill.

(7) Train your self to pray for the sake of praying:

Saint Isaac was asked: "How do we learn to pray?" and he answered: "By praying."

There is no doubt that prayer, like any spiritual activity, *"comes down from the Father of lights."* (James 1:17). Seek it as did the disciples who said: *"Lord, teach us to pray."* (Luke 11:1).

Say to Him: Allow me, O'Lord, to pray, and the sweet seclusion to be with You. Give me the words that I should say and grant me the desire to pray. Grant me love with which to love You and which makes me pray. Grant me warmth in prayer, tears and submission. I do not know how to pray, O'Lord, so teach me how. Grant me the appropriate feelings for prayer. Speak to me, O'Lord, that I may speak with You.

(8) Train yourself to pray for others:

Do not only pray for yourself when you fast, but also pray for others. How many people have asked you to pray for them and you did not? Try to remember during your fast, those whom you feel are in need of prayer because of a problem, hardship, sickness or in need of it for their spiritual life. Pray for them as well as for those who have departed.

Pray for the Church, for the safety of the country, for the general welfare, for those who do not know God, for the heretics, the reckless, and the infidels, and for God's Kingdom on earth.

It is a good opportunity that you pray for others, especially for the following:

(9) Pray for your offenders:

This is more of a divine order than instructions. Thus, the Lord says: *"Pray for those who spitefully use you and persecute you."* (Matt 5:44). It is an opportunity for you to train yourself in carrying out this commandment while you fast.

Pray that God may forgive your offenders and save them. Pray for their love to you and your love for them so that your heart may not change towards them because of their offence. Wish them well and pray to God to have Him spare you from condemning them in thought or before others.

It is natural that you pray for those whom you love but it is much more pleasant to pray for those who have offend you.

Say to Him: O'Lord protect, rescue and forgive them. Grant me a blessing in their eyes. Make me to love them as much as I love those who are dear to me. Make my heart pure towards them.

(10) Other drills for prayer:

(a) Train yourself to pray early in the morning and to have God as the first one to talk, even for a short prayer every day saying to him, Thank You, O'Lord and bless this day. And grant me a sacred day that I may please You.

(b) Train yourself in repeating prayers of saints. Look for them and use them in praying. (The prayers of Prophets are found in the bible and in the Church book of the Joyous Holy Saturday).

(c) Read spiritual books that bear spiritual warmth that help you pray in earnest.

(d) Pray before doing any work, and before every visit and every meeting.

Other spiritual drills:

a.   Train yourself in spiritual readings:

Religious readings are numerous and limitless. However, sacred fasting days, should not be used to read books that increase your knowledge as much as the ones of worship. Concentrate on spiritual books that inflame your heart with God's love, stimulate you, leading you to prayer, and urge you to repent and lead a life of purity. Such should be your reading material to stimulate you in a spiritual way. As for other religious books, I do not forbid you to use them. However, they come second in a fast, while spiritual books and biographies of saints take priority.

b.   Train yourself in church hymns and melodies:

This is especially so in hymns and melodies that have the

spirit of prayer, in which you feel you are communicating with God, which you recite from the heart and the soul, and which touch your emotions and affect your heart.

Try to memorise the hymns that move you and repeat them often.

c.   Train yourself also in prostration:

If you neglect it at other times, be careful to observe it while fasting.

Drills in certain virtues:

It is possible to benefit by profound spiritual feelings that you may experiences while fasting. This may allow a person to gain any virtue that his heart longs for. This may include tolerance, forbearance, calmness, meekness, being cautious, respect for others, generosity, honesty in work, righteousness, discipline, etc.

If you came out of every fast well versed in one virtue, it would be of great spiritual gain for you.

Table of Contents

www.ingramcontent.com/pod-product-compliance
Lightning Source LLC
Chambersburg PA
CBHW050947030426

42339CB00007B/326